Penguin in the Pew

(2.0)

By

D.C. Parris

Linux is a trademark of Linus Torvalds. All other trademarks are the property of their respective owners.

A portion of the author's royalties are given to support the free and open source advocacy ministry of *Oakdale Christian Fellowship*

Written by Donald C. Parris

dcparris@matheteuo.org or don.parris@thefreelyproject.org

Front cover & image editing by Stanley Petrowski

Volunteer Editorial Team:

Stan Glasoe
John Lamb
Vince Littler
Mike McMullin
James Pryor

Published through:
Lulu Enterprises, Inc.
3131 RDU Center Dr., Ste. 210
Morrisville, NC 27560

Version 2.0

Dedication

To the entire MIS Staff of National Gypsum Company, especially Gary Potts, who so patiently answered my questions in the beginning.

And to To Ben, Bob, Linc, & Tim, my co-laborers in Christ

TABLE OF CONTENTS

i

FOREWORD TO THE
SECOND EDITION

Since the first edition of Penguin in the Pew hit the web in May 2004, much has changed. The GNU/Linux operating system itself, and the many applications that accompany it, have matured tremendously since the 2.4 kernel I was using at the time. I have discovered a much larger cache of programs available for Christians and churches than I believed existed. And there is a visible community of believers who are ready, willing, and able to assist other believers and ministries seeking to explore the world of free and open source software.

When I first wrote "Penguin in the Pew" I lamented the lack of good software for churches, and for Christians in general. Shortly after releasing it on the Internet, people began to bring to my attention all kinds of free and open source software for the universal Church. Bible study tools, lyrics projection, website builders, distance education tools for missions organizations, and even church management applications have quite a history. FOSS Bible applications support 60 translations across some thirty languages on GNU/Linux, Mac, and Windows, and have been downloaded tens of thousands of times.

OpenOffice.org and the Mozilla Internet tools, Firefox and Thunderbird, are quickly outstripping the most popular proprietary solutions in the same fields. Remote desktop sharing makes remote support simple, and is literally a matter of a couple of clicks. Multimedia tools that run on GNU/Linux are quickly proving themselves in a number of churches.

For users who depend on graphical installation and configuration tools, the tool sets offered by many GNU/Linux distributions have definitely come a long way. The Linux kernel itself is more mature. The number of so-called "Live" GNU/Linux distributions that offer worry-free trials and ease of installation is growing. Hardware auto-detection works better than ever. There is seamless support for a broad range of peripherals, such as cameras, scanners, and USB mass storage devices.

Perhaps the most spectacular thing to happen in the wake of "Penguin in the Pew" and the articles is the coalescing of a community of Believers who use free and open source software (FOSS). Hundreds of believers from around the world have been coming together to develop, use, and advocate FOSS, and to provide technical support for Christians and ministries. This growing community is on the verge of breaking loose in the real world, as they are also beginning to meet in person, and not just on the web. The once barely visible community is now a vibrant community consisting of Christians from around the world.

The opening chapter, "Linux isn't ready yet? Says Who?", has been changed to "A Legal and Moral Dilemma". The question now is not whether GNU/Linux is ready, but whether the church is ready? The answer depends largely on a given user or organization. The attitudes that people hold play the most important role in the exploration process. The real question each individual and organization must ask is, "are we ready to take advantage of an established technology built on a community development platform?

FOSS has traditionally been better known for its robustness, stability and strong security, rather than for its ease of use. FOSS solutions, while still robust, secure, and stable, offer a more polished look and feel that makes users more comfortable. Most of the graphical desktops look similar to, and even behave the same as, Microsoft Windows and Mac OS X. Applications look and feel similar to their Windows counterparts. Many applications include wizard-like utilities to help users get up and running.

That I have expanded this edition by more than double the original number of pages reflects my growing understanding of the issues involved as well as of the software available for Christians and ministries. I have sought to help readers understand how they can benefit from and participate in the Christian FOSS community. I have also addressed more issues that some new users might find a little puzzling, notably the GNU/Linux filesystem.

This book discusses legal and philosophical issues in some depth. However, nothing in this book should be construed as legal advice. Nor should anything herein be construed as endorsing licenses that prohibit sharing. I suggest that some Christian churches may use proprietary software illegally. This should not be construed as direct accusations, but is intended to open the eyes of the Church to potential issues in many ministries. It is up to individual ministries to investigate the legality of the software they use.

I am deeply indebted to many people for the content of this book. Greg, whose unfulfilled promise of 24/7 technical support forced me to learn more than I originally sought to know about computers. He sold me my first PC and helped me to overcome my technophobia. Gary Potts, of National Gypsum, tirelessly answered my questions when I first began to use computers. Robert Miller has answered questions about software development. Indeed, the entire IT staff of National Gypsum has made this book possible – despite being Windows administrators.

I am also grateful to the wonderful folks who participate so much on the SUSE Linux e-mail lists – they are my teachers and my greatest critics. Likewise, my brothers and sisters in the Christian free and open source software community have contributed much to my understanding of GNU/Linux and have even supported many of my advocacy efforts. James Pryor and Mike McMullin contributed much to my discussion of free software philosophy and the legal foundation of Copyright Law.

Of course, were it not for the efforts of Christians who have devoted many years to developing software for the Church, I would have had little use to expand this book. Many in the Christian free and open source software community have encouraged and supported this endeavor. Thanks to folks like Troy Griffits and the Crosswire Bible Society, the New American Standard Bible module is now available for the Sword Project applications.

I should also thank Richard Stallman, whose foresight years ago prepared the way for people to be able to run computers on nothing but free software. His willingness to explain – and patience in answering my dozens of questions is more than some might expect. His input has helped clarify my own understanding of free software, thus enhancing my ability to discuss the Free Software Foundation and the GNU Project with some degree of accuracy.

It is my prayer that you will find this book intriguing, informative and compelling. I hope you will come to see, as I do, that free and open source software is the best software for your church. If this book does nothing else, I hope it at least helps you to understand that it is not necessary to spend hundreds of dollars on software – and worse, promise not to share it with your neighbor - when there are software licenses that encourage you to share. This is truly Christian.

"What the Messiah has freed us for is freedom! Therefore, stand firm, and don't let yourselves be tied up again to a yoke of slavery." - *The Complete Jewish Bible*

Don Parris

Charlotte, NC

ABOUT THIS BOOK

This book is intended to introduce church and non-profit leaders, as well as Information Technology consultants who work with such organizations to the idea of using the GNU/Linux operating system, as well as free and open source software solutions in general within religious and non-profit organizations. While intended for the folks involved in their church's information technology ministry, the rest of the Christians in the pews stand to gain much as well.

While I have endeavored to make this booklet easy for the non-technical church leaders in the crowd, many will probably find at least some technological background helpful. If you already have an idea of what an operating system is or does, as compared to a particular application, such as a word processor, you'll probably be o.k. If you understand any networking or system administration issues, you'll be even better off. That said I am including a glossary, and notes within the body of the book, for those who may not have even a basic understanding of many of the terms used.

We start off by examining a situation that many organizations need to consider, licensing and the moral issue of using software in violation of typical proprietary software license agreements. We then get a brief overview of the various challenges an organization might face in migrating to the GNU/Linux platform. Each challenge is tackled individually, followed by a discussion about getting technical support and developing practical migration strategies.

I have expanded the Linux background and also included a discussion of the state of the Christian FOSS community, which is growing ever larger and more vocal. Thousands of Christians from various denominational and national backgrounds are discovering and deploying free and open source software solutions, and hundreds are participating in the active community. Many of the Christians involved in the community are home users, or simply desire to help their church. For this reason, even the average Christian will find this to be a useful book.

Ultimately, readers will discover what free and open source software is, how it will benefit them, what challenges they need to overcome, and that there is a community with a broad knowledge base ready, willing and able to support churches and ministries seeking to migrate to these alternatives.

Illustration 1- Lyricue in use in the developer's church, Gosford Baptist Church in Gosford Australia.

This book was produced using OpenOffice.org 1.1.3 running on SUSE Linux 9.2 Professional. Screenshots were created using Ksnapshot, the GNOME panel screenshot applet, and The Gimp. The front cover was produced using Blender 3D and The Gimp.

1. A LITTLE BACKGROUND

FOR "NON-TECHIES"

Many folks who use computers understand very little about the computer itself. I have encountered many people that do not understand the difference between the operating system and the applications that run on the operating system. If you happen to be one of these folks, you should probably check out this section. You technologists, on the other hand, will likely want to skip to the next section.

Simply put, the operating system is what makes the computer tick. The operating system handles all the details of interacting with the hardware so the application programs don't have to worry about that as much. For example, as long as all the programs know how to interact with the operating system, they don't have to know how to interact with the printer, because the operating system does that for them. The kernel is the heart of the operating system, and is what handles most of this interaction with the hardware.

Table 1 (next page) shows a few common operating systems, what hardware they run on, and how they are typically used. Most people use one of two operating systems at home and in their businesses, at least in the cubicles and offices. Microsoft Windows is the most commonly used system of all, and runs on the IBM PC and compatibles. Apple's Mac OS X runs on Apple's MacIntosh computers, more commonly referred to simply as "Macs".

Hardware	Operating System	Predominant Use
Mac (Apple)	Apple Mac OSX	Graphics & Printing & Home Use
IBM PC	Microsoft Windows	Home & Office Desktop
IBM PC	GNU/Linux & BSD	Business Networks & Enthusiasts
Sun SPARC	Sun Solaris	Business Networks

What many people do not realize is that two alternatives to Mac OS X and Windows exist, having spread mostly by word of mouth. One is called GNU, which uses the Linux kernel. The other is known as BSD, which is actually the foundation of Mac OS X. The Linux kernel is the best known part of the GNU system, and many simply refer to GNU/Linux as "Linux" out of convenience[1]. This book uses the term "GNU" or "GNU/Linux", except when referring to the kernel specifically, as it seems strange to refer to a whole operating system by its kernel.

GNU/Linux is said to be a "UNIX-like" operating system. While it is not recognized by the standards body that defines UNIX systems, it does adhere to the UNIX standards and is like UNIX in nearly every respect. Unlike Windows or Mac, which have only one form, GNU/Linux and BSD exist in a variety of flavors or *distributions*. There are, in fact, over 330 active GNU/Linux distributions. GNU/Linux is mostly used as a server operating system, but is also being used increasingly as a workstation operating system.

---

1   It makes more sense to this author to use "GNU" when referring to the complete system. Most users do not refer to Microsoft Windows as "ntkernel32.exe". However, a great many people have taken to calling GNU "Linux".

Some GNU/Linux distributions serve the general purposes of most home and business uses. Many of these are specialized toward a specific purpose, such as firewalls or evaluation CDs that people can run without installing the operating system on their computer. The live CD let's users get a feel for a GNU/Linux system's capabilities. Other distributions are geared towards hobbyists who want to learn how GNU/Linux works.

BSD is actually UNIX, and this author knows of at least three or four main variants. The best-known are FreeBSD, OpenBSD, and NetBSD. There are at least six other BSD distributions out there. You may be interested to know that FreeBSD is the underlying system for the easy-to-use Mac OS X. Microsoft may still use FreeBSD servers for some of its websites as well. MSN (or Hotmail) used to be hosted on BSD.

These operating systems were designed from the ground up to serve as multi-user systems capable of operating in a network environment. Many applications (programs typically used by end-users) exist for GNU and BSD. From office suites that open Microsoft Office documents to musical notation editors to DVD players, users can find applications that will enable them to accomplish much in their church or other non-profit organization. And because these systems almost always include the all the tools users need to develop their own software, there is always the opportunity to customize your software or develop your own.

One advantage of these systems is that they work well in the "client-server" infrastructure in which one computer provides services for another. The best example is of the Internet, where web servers retrieve web pages for web clients (your browser). Another good example is using a file server to store files you create at your workstation. Client-server terminology might seem a bit confusing, as the concept applies not only to physical computers, but also to programs.

The illustration above provides a rough idea of what client-server computing is. Typically, the server resides in a secure closet or room, and is rarely touched unless administrators need to perform maintenance tasks. The server could be running Apache, and or a number of other server programs. The workstation is the tool for users to access the information or services, such as printing or file storage, on the server.

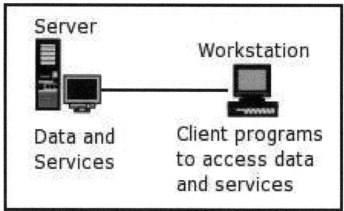

Illustration 2 - The client-server concept – the server provides data and services which are typically accessed using client software on a remote workstation.

The fact is that a single computer can be both the client and the server, depending on the situation. For instance, a single computer can run both, the server and the client programs, such as the MySQL database server and its clients. In another case, one workstation can store files for another, and vice versa. In other words, Joe may give Sally access to files stored on his computer, while also being able to access files on her computer. This is typically called a peer-to-peer setup.

Are you thoroughly confused now? If so, don't sweat it too much. Some of this stuff is just hard to picture. Just know that in client-server computing, one computer or program provides services to another computer or program. This book will refer to servers (computers) and workstations (client computers) when referring to the hardware, and to servers and clients (client programs) when referring to software.

Many organizations around the United States refurbish old computers and load one version or another of GNU/Linux on them to give to low-income families. Some churches are already using GNU/Linux to provide network services to Windows workstations. Others are using it to host websites or intranets. Some are using it for the cost savings alone. One church denomination's headquarters in Germany uses SUSE Linux Open Exchange Server to serve more than 20,000 users.

One major difference between GNU/Linux and Windows is the filesystem. For starters, some non-techies may be confused by the term "directories" if they've been using "folders". Folders are typically referred to as "directories", which is the way everyone used to refer to them anyway. Microsoft adopted Apple's terminology, when they launched Windows 95, with a goal of simplifying the terminology for new users. So the terms 'folder' and 'directory' are synonymous.

Many Windows users are familiar with the c:\ prompt, which denotes the root directory of the hard drive. Windows 95 introduced the "My Documents" and "Program Files" folders. Windows 2000 and XP places the My Documents folder under the "Documents and Settings" folder. Most programs should be stored in the My Programs folder, while users store their documents in the My Documents folder.

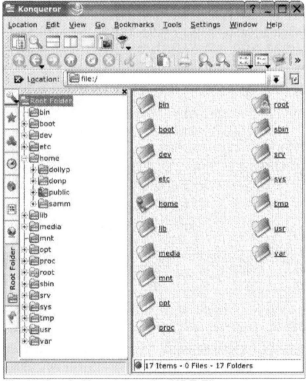

Illustration 3- Konqueror, the KDE File manager
showing the root filesystem and 3 home directories

Illustration 3 shows a file manager, similar to Windows Explorer. GNU/Linux, along with most UNIX systems, uses a "/" to represent the root directory.

Underneath / is a fairly complex, but logical directory structure. The image on the next page shows three users and a public directory where all users can put shared files. It also shows the main directories under /. We'll address the filesystem in more depth later in the book. For now, you should just bear this basic information in mind.

Most operating systems also have two types of *shells*. The shell is simply the starting point for everything a user does on the computer. A shell can either be a command-line or a graphical shell. The command-line gives you a simple "$:" or "c:\" or something similar, while it waits for you to enter commands. After typing a command, you hit the "Enter" key to make something happen. Bash (Bourne Again Shell) is the most commonly used command-line shell in GNU/Linux systems. Other shells are available for GNU/Linux and BSD systems. You have the same command-line capability under Windows, but only one shell. The image below shows what the filesystem looks like in the Bash shell.

```
donp@luke:~> cd /
donp@luke:/> ls
bin   dev   home   media   opt    root   srv   tmp   var
boot  etc   lib    mnt     proc   sbin   sys   usr
donp@luke:/> █
```

Illustration 4 - The root filesystem from the command line

The graphical shell – also known as a desktop – is just a pretty picture for all you do at the command-line. Instead of having to remember the name of the command that launches your word processor, you click a little icon to make it start. But you can still type in

7

the name of the command at the command prompt to make it start, if you want to. In modern times, the command-line is used for system administration tasks, while the graphical shell is used for productivity tasks.

Illustration 5 - The KDE desktop, shown here as part of SUSE Linux 9.2, is similar to the Windows desktop.

The image on the previous page shows the KDE graphical shell under GNU/Linux. If you pay close attention, you may be able to see just how similar KDE is to the Windows desktop. A few desktop icons clutter the left side. The Start menu is the big green icon on the far left of the task bar. The launcher tray, task bar, and system tray function similarly to their Windows counterparts. The numbered squares in the task bar are the virtual desktops. Clicking one takes you to a different KDE desktop.

Windows and Mac OS X are both proprietary and their use is governed by the developers' software licenses. Similarly, many of the applications that run on each have proprietary licenses. Proprietary licenses (except for proprietary freeware) usually prohibit sharing the software with other users, although many people still do so in violation of the law.

GNU and BSD, on the other hand, have licenses that do allow users to share their copies with others. Most of the applications that run on these two operating systems also have similar licenses. The licenses offer additional freedoms, something we discuss in more detail throughout the book.

There is a subtle distinction between free software and open source software. The distinction lies in the fact that free software propagates the freedom of the end-users, and essentially forces developers to offer derivative works under the same license. Open source software allows the developer to release derivatives under a proprietary license. This means that while all free software is open source, not all open source software is necessarily free software.

In most cases, I have used the term "FOSS" or "free and open source software" to refer to the whole category. Where the term "open source software" is used in this book, "free software" should be considered a sub-category of open source.

2. A LEGAL AND MORAL

DILEMMA

The pastor needed to upgrade his church's office computer. A deacon suggested he had a copy of a popular proprietary operating system as well as a proprietary office suite that he could bring in and install. I suggested giving GNU/Linux a try - after all, it came (at that time) with StarOffice 5.2[2]. I had been using Mandrake Linux 8.0, and even offered to install and configure the system. The deacon responded that he had talked with an IT guy on his job, and he didn't think GNU/Linux was "quite ready just yet". The pastor settled for his deacon's assessment and solution.

This encounter raises some important issues pertaining to the decision-making process. First, they failed to understand the issues and to get the facts. Second, they passed up the opportunity to expand their horizons. Third, they potentially placed their church in legal jeopardy, namely due to copyright law – a truly costly error. Let's examine these issues in depth.

The deacon had not experienced GNU/Linux for himself. He had simply parroted someone else's opinion. Whether that "technician" had experience with GNU/Linux is not known. I had actual experience with both GNU/Linux and the legacy system they were currently using. The fact is that many companies, especially small and home-based businesses, were

---

2   Note that StarOffice is non-free software. OpenOffice.org, which is derived from StarOffice is free software.

---

already deploying GNU/Linux on their desktops. The pastor accepted hearsay in favor of experiential knowledge. Had he taken an hour or two, given me the chance to demonstrate GNU/Linux for him and/or his staff, he would have been able to make a more informed decision.

From a theological perspective, this pastor missed a phenomenal opportunity to demonstrate for his sheep the ability to adapt to new things, to break free of the old ways of thinking. This is a battle that church leaders face in every arena. Whether it's the style of worship or which activities to start and end this year, churches face the decision of moving from their comfort zones and into the realm of faith. As pastors, we teach our congregations that stewardship applies to every aspect of life. Hence, we must set an example of how to face new challenges wisely and intelligently.

On top of all this, he may have inadvertently encouraged the illegal use of software. Based on the conversation, it is unfortunately possible that the deacon could have violated copyright laws in using the proprietary OS. Depending on how the church is organized, he and the deacon – potentially the whole church – could have been held liable for the copyright violations. One business had to settle for $100,000 because they "thought" they were "o.k." with their proprietary software. Incidentally, they now use open source software exclusively.

The U.S. Constitution allows for copyright law and is intended to provide a balance between the rights of the author, artist, or developer, and the general public. Copyright is not a constitutional right, nor even recognized as "natural" law. Copyright grants these authors exclusive rights to control their work. At the same time, these rights are limited, both in terms of time and in terms of use. For instance, copyright is limited to 70 years after the author's death, and people can quote small amounts of material for use in criticism and similar endeavors.

Software is copyrighted unless the developer explicitly places it into the public domain. Most commercial software is copyrighted, and includes a license that specifies the user's rights. These typically include the right to run the program, and to keep a back-up copy. Users typically have no right to modify, copy or redistribute the program. This means it is illegal to copy or share software with your neighbor, unless the license explicitly permits such actions.

The case above involves a church member who may have contributed software to the church in violation of the EULA and copyright law. Loaning your proprietary software CD to your neighbor usually involves the same kind of violation. The fact is that many people, including Christians, do share software and other materials frequently – in spite of the legal constraints. Sharing is not immoral, but breaking the terms of the license would be.

Herein lies the problem of a non-free license – it attempts to prohibit sharing and/or modification by the user. This is unnatural for Christians – and people of most other faiths – for whom the primary expression of God's love is through giving and sharing. Free software is a technological ram in the bush that offers users and developers alike a business model that does not prohibit sharing.

We don't know how many churches use the same faulty thinking when considering their software options. However, a Christian, living in New Orleans, recently wrote that he knew of a church with several computers, but that only one of those had properly licensed software. Setting aside any possible legal challenges involved, one can only wonder in amazement that the Bride of Christ – the Church – would use proprietary software in an illegal manner. Imagine our Heavenly Father's displeasure at the notion.

Some churches think they have to have the latest and greatest in software technology. In fact, many churches may not realize that the "latest and greatest" software is not even proprietary. Some churches refuse to change on account of "our current software is easy to use". That is not to say that FOSS alternatives are not easy to use. The real issue is simply that they are comfortable with what they have.

The church needs to realize that "ease of use", while certainly important, is not the only basis for making decisions – especially when a morally compelling reason for changing is presented. It is difficult to imagine a more compelling reason to change than the desire to obey Christ's command to love our neighbors as ourselves. Proprietary software makes this prohibitive at best. Free and open source software, by their very nature, encourage Christians to love their neighbors by enabling them to share.

I have suggested that churches using proprietary software illegally is a disgrace to God only to have people suggest that the current software is "easy to use" – as if that justifies breaking the law and disgracing our Lord's name. It is sad that people just throw their hands up in the air, and say, "well, we can't migrate – the proprietary software is just too easy to use". I can just picture Jesus now, "sorry, Father, but I'm used to being human now. I've never been up on a cross before. I've heard it's agonizing. I'm just too set in my ways."

Furthermore, if "ease of use" is the only factor considered in the decision-making process, then the technological and moral issues are ignored to the detriment of the church. The most important free software is relatively easy to use. Even so, does "ease of use" actually outweigh the moral challenges of being forced into dependence upon someone else? Doe "ease of use" outweigh the freedom and the moral imperative to love our neighbors, as expressed through giving and sharing?

The Business Software Alliance is an organization that enforces software licensing violations in the business arena. They have also gone after private schools. Although I do not know of any churches being pursued by the BSA, churches are not above the law. Violators could face statutory damages from the license holder of up to $150,000 per program copied, along with other financial considerations. Additionally, violators can then be criminally prosecuted and face fines up to $250,000 and jail time[3].

Ideally, churches using proprietary software (regardless of the legality of the license) will replace it

---

3*http://www.bsa.org/usa/antipiracy/Piracy-and-the-Law.cfm

as soon as possible with free and open source alternatives. Not only can they pass along copies of free and open source software to poorer members of their congregations, they will experience freedom on a level they never thought possible. In the long run, they will be better able to help others in vastly more ways than is now possible, by moving to free and open source software. Once your ministry has migrated, your improved financial stewardship will simply be a secondary benefit.

All of this has implications for you and your church. Do you understand the issues involved? Are you willing to consider facts rather than hearsay? This book will help you, as a church leader, to better understand the basic issues that churches should address when considering their computing platform.

3. IDENTIFYING THE ISSUES

So you've discovered that, due to costs, security, or legal issues, you may need to change your software. Before you rush down to the church office and start revamping, there are a few things you need to consider. The major issues are compatibility and interoperability, usability, freedom, and cost. In addition, the power, flexibility, and stability your computing platform offers deserve consideration. We'll examine each of these in more depth, but I would like to help you see the big picture.

When I speak of compatibility, churches need to assess whether GNU/Linux will work with their current hardware and any church administration software they might use. Most, but not all hardware works with GNU/Linux. You might just be surprised how much hardware is supported by GNU/Linux. As for church management software, there is no software that is compatible with common programs, such as ACS, PowerChurch or Servant Keeper. However, you can still migrate your data, which is a more tedious task than it is complex.

Interoperability refers to the ability of GNU/Linux and its applications to function well with other operating systems and their applications. GNU/Linux does very well with this, and many free and open source applications work well with their proprietary counterparts. For instance, you can open Word documents in Writer, the OpenOffice.org word processor. You can also connect your GNU/Linux system to other operating systems.

The question of usability involves the "intuitiveness", or "ease of use" of the interface you work with. Some consider GNU/Linux to be "difficult" or not as "user-friendly" to use as other operating systems. One test has established that neither GNU/Linux nor Windows is any more intuitive than the other, where new computer users are concerned. It is important to note that this issue is almost purely subjective. The fact is that we tend to stick with what we are used to because we are comfortable with that.

When we speak of freedom in the software realm, we refer to the user's right to use or modify the software obtained (be it cost-free or purchased) to suit their needs. Proprietary Software generally limits the user to running the software on a specified number of machines and does not permit adaptation to the users needs except according to the options programmed by the supplier. However, open source software generally allows the user to run it on as many machines as he desires and also allows anyone the right to modify any aspect of the program to meet a particular need.

> *"The free software philosophy rejects a specific widespread business practice, but it is not against business. When businesses respect the users' freedom, we wish them success."*
>
> *- Richard M. Stallman "The GNU Project"*
> (http://www.gnu.org/gnu/thegnuproject.html)

Freedom from "vendor lock-in" puts the customer in charge of the pricing. A number of churches and other organizations seem to feel that migrating to free and open source software would be too costly. This should be your first clue that you really need to migrate. The initial cost of a migration could, in fact, be more expensive. However, even in those rare cases that this is true, the long-term impact is still to reduce your overall cost of computing.

For example, suppose you could migrate from Microsoft Windows to IBM Windows to save money, that would encourage competition among Windows vendors. Unfortunately, there is only one Windows, and it costs about the same at OfficeMax as it does at Office Depot. In the GNU/Linux world, customers can choose from several vendors with a variety of system options and services. A variety of prices across commercial GNU/Linux distributions reflects the highly competitive marketplace.

As for power and flexibility, GNU/Linux runs on practically every hardware platform. From Sharp Zaurus hand-helds to floppy-based network routers to 64-bit operating systems to IBM mainframes, GNU/Linux will run it all. That older hardware you still have hanging around will make a great (and cheap) network terminal, or even an e-mail or fax server. With over 330 active distributions to choose from, you won't be locked into a single vendor. In fact, you can choose between non-commercial or commercial distributions.

We'll also examine costs, an important factor in the decision-making process. After all, the church must have the facts to be an effective steward of her resources. The cost of migration is a hotly debated issue. To make matters a bit more interesting, a number of factors can affect the actual cost. How much will it cost to purchase GNU/Linux? How much will it cost to train our staff? Will we need to hire a tech guy?

When it comes to power, GNU/Linux errs on the side of offering far more power than is immediately necessary for the typical end user. Or does it? Consider the rapidly growing church that has 50 members today, but by next year grows to 150 members. Trust me when I say that GNU/Linux and one of the included SQL database servers can handle the data for thousands of members before it even starts thinking about breaking a sweat. So you've got plenty of room to grow.

We must bear in mind that "with freedom comes responsibility". We have the responsibility to administer our computers, and in a secure manner. It is our responsibility to secure our computers and our networks from external attacks and viruses. It is our responsibility to ensure a back-up procedure that is capable of helping us to recover from security breaches and other failures. Part of that responsibility entails learning a few new skills.

Freedom also means that we need more knowledge to better understand the choices we face. GNU/Linux not only offers freedom, but flexibility to boot. Which desktop environment should you use? Which web server should you run? Do you have the need to run Oracle's SAP 9 with its tremendous memory requirements? Or can you get by with MySQL? Many pastors may not realize that I am speaking of databases – and that's OK.

I am not asking you to know it all right now. Think about it. Did you understand the depths of John 3:16 when you first received the Gospel? Of course not! So why reject GNU/Linux simply on the grounds that you do not fully understand it? As you have taken years to explore your faith, so you should time to explore GNU/Linux. Will it be easy? There will be challenges.

Then again, simply upgrading from one version of Windows to another can cause problems. GNU/Linux often does a better job of correctly identifying and configuring a printer than some operating systems – at least in my experience. The only problem I ever had was configuring a printer across my ministry's GNU/Linux network. Along with my personal experience, I've heard numerous complaints about setting up printers with a certain popular operating system!

In other words, migrating from Windows 98 to Windows XP brings change. There are new features to learn. Migrating from Windows to the KDE desktop brings change. Simply put, some things are different. That alone has scared some people half to death. They are not necessarily more difficult, just different. And you say you would follow Jesus to the cross? Hang with me. We have much to discover. Let's look at some facts that just might make this cross a bit more appealing.

Having introduced you to the challenges you'll face, and how to overcome them, I'll also point out the most prominent applications that churches can use. I'll also introduce you around the community. You should know where to go when you need help, and where to find applications or how to get help introducing free and open source software to your church and local community.

4. TRULY FREE COMPUTING

In the beginning was the source code, and the source code was free. Computer programmers (mostly scientists) frequently shared their code to help each other out. It was the way of the world in those days. Then some people decided to make the code proprietary – that is, they held back the code. In holding back the code, they brought an end to the sharing community.

Source code is the code the programmer actually writes when developing a program. As it stands, source code just sits there. When it is translated into binary format, which the computer understands, the computer can "run" it as a program. In the beginning, people simply passed source code around to help each other out. They shared it, gave it away. Anyone who received it could modify it for their purposes.

> "...But interest in the software is growing faster than awareness of the philosophy it is based on, and this leads to trouble. Our ability to meet the challenges and threats described above depends on the will to stand firm for freedom. To make sure our community has this will, we need to spread the idea to the new users as they come into the community." – Richard Stallman, "The GNU Project" (http://www.gnu.org/gnu/thegnuproject.html)

That changed when folks got clever, and decided to distribute only the binary program, while keeping the source code. Companies began to require developers (a fancy word for programmers) to sign non-disclosure agreements (NDAs) and end-users to sign End-User License Agreements (EULAs). This prevented the users from being able to modify it. It also gave developers greater control over the program.

> *"...This meant that the first step in using a computer was to promise not to help your neighbor. A cooperating community was forbidden. The rule made by the owners of proprietary software was, "If you share with your neighbor, you are a pirate. If you want any changes, beg us to make them." – Richard Stallman, "The GNU Project"*
> *(http://www.gnu.org/gnu/thegnuproject.html)*

Many end users (who tend to know little about programming) were happy to give up their rights to modify the program. To them, it was a simple trade-off. Pay a lot of money; let the developer modify the program. It's a pretty simple equation. However, they gave up their rights, not only to modify the program, but also to redistribute (share) the program with others. What's more, by declining their rights to the source code, they chose to place a great deal of trust in the developer's hands.

The Moral Foundation of Free Software

I am not a programmer. Having the right to modify the code would seem to be of little use to me because of that. Even so, if I have access to it, I may be able to find someone to modify it for me. There might be some minor things I *can* do to make the program work more the way I want it. For instance, having the source code allows me to re-compile the program to perhaps take advantage of certain features of my system.

This is a little more technically advanced than many users want to get. Frankly, some might be surprised to discover just how simple compiling a program can be – even if it seems a little geeky. Still, it points to the notion that having access to the source code is important for very practical reasons. Having access to source code is not a pie-in-the-sky ideal that has no application to non-geeks; rather it is a very practical way to exercise control over your system – regardless of your status as a "non-techie".

Actually, I have helped contribute to a few development projects in small ways, such as suggesting changes, which the developers made. This kind of participation benefits everyone. Frequently, if you want a change, many others will also. Some of those others who want the same changes you want are programmers. They will make the change and share it with you. Many people have no way to participate (i.e, due to lack of Internet connection or other issues) and still benefit from the contributions of others.

A great many computer programs nowadays are free, as in free coffee, but not free as in freedom. The developers give you a program that you can run. What they don't tell you might just hurt you. Many tell their users in tiny (never mind the "fine" print), legalistic mumbo jumbo print that their program includes software that detects everything you do on your computer – other than spilling coffee on the keyboard.

This raises a question. How far do you trust your software vendor? Some well-respected proprietary vendors actually have reputations for underhandedness. Regardless of how far you trust your vendor, if the code is proprietary, your trust rests on a sandy foundation. Again, having access to the source code is a very practical matter. Access to the source code guarantees you can determine the suitability of the code to run on your system, even if you need to find an outside consultant.

The problem with trusting the developer is that some developers operate in an immoral manner, even while they may comply with the law. Furthermore, since only developers have access to their proprietary code, they are the only ones – apart from outlaw hackers (better known as "crackers") who will know if the code is actually secure. In a free or open source software program, everyone has access to the source, thus security vulnerabilities are found and fixed far more quickly as a general rule.

> *"The payoff from having secret bits is well understood; traditionally, software business models have been constructed around it. Until recently, the payoff from independent peer review was not well understood. The Linux operating system, however, drives home a lesson that we should probably have learned years ago from the history of the Internet's core software and other branches of engineering—that open-source peer review is the only scalable method for achieving high reliability and quality." - Eric S. Raymond, The Cathedral and the Bazaar, Revised Edition, Section 4.10.1*

I mentioned the "right" to redistribute (share) the program with others. Scripturally speaking, Jesus commanded us to love our neighbors. Throughout the entire Bible, such love is demonstrated through giving and sharing. The Non-Disclosure Agreements and End-User License Agreements that accompany most proprietary software prohibit access to the source code and the act of redistribution. This prohibition is artificial – not natural – and contradicts the teaching of Jesus Christ (and many others).

Some will argue that the Scripture is also replete with passages about being rewarded for one's labor. We should not "muzzle the ox", as it were. However, this argument ignores the fact that free and open source software can be sold. It also ignores the benefit – to both, users and developers – of the collaborative development model. Ironically, most developers are paid, not from the sale of software, but from the internal use of software they develop for their employers.

For instance, I may sell a word processor under a free software license. You purchase it and pass along a copy to your neighbor. Your neighbor improves it, and then redistributes the modified version. The free software license allows both of us to benefit from your neighbor's contribution – along with everyone else. We all benefit from the re-use of the source code, as none of us has to reinvent the wheel to develop our software. Thus, I benefit directly from making my code "open".

> *"When I speak at technical conferences, I usually begin my talk by asking two questions: how many in the audience are paid to write software, and for how many do their salaries depend on the sale value of software. I generally get a forest of hands for the first question, few or none for the second, and considerable audience surprise at the proportion."* - Eric S. Raymond, The Cathedral and the Bazaar, Section 4.3

The Open Development Model

In his book, <u>The Cathedral and the Bazaar,</u> Eric S. Raymond argues that 75% of a programmer's job lies in the maintenance of the software developed. He further argues that most programmers are paid to develop software in-house, and that their code is thus difficult to copy or re-use. Additionally, if a proprietary software vendor closes its doors, the customer is left holding a bag of non-maintainable software.

Many have also argued that developers have a right to get paid for their work. Thus, if they wish to charge a "per seat" fee for licenses, and restrict the redistribution of their software, that is o.k. They argue that it is not *always* proper to help others, by referring to the act of helping criminals. However, to my knowledge, no one has a right to prevent me from sharing with my non-criminal neighbor. It may be legal, in some countries, to prohibit sharing, but so are many things that violate the conscience of many Christians.

We know that the rain falls on the just and the unjust alike. Thus, many software businesses have made a handsome profit from making the act of sharing a crime. On the other hand, the users have been complicit in such profitability by agreeing to not help their neighbors. Part of the problem lies in the attempt to sell software as if it were shovels or some other physical good. Free and open source software requires a different business model, but only for those businesses that engage primarily selling software.

The new model involves distributing software (either by download or by ordering CDs), and providing technical support, consulting, and other anciliary services. There is no restriction on the redistribution of the software, but the professional technical support is limited to those who have purchased it. Likewise, many people purchase manuals to help them learn the new software. Many folks actually purchase software, even though they can download it for free, because they appreciate the value they get.

I refer to this as a new "software economy". I have pointed out elsewhere in this book that many businesses have learned to profit from this (relatively) new model. In the long term, it is a business model that acknowledges users' freedom, while simultaneously enabling people to profit from their labor. Those businesses that do not adapt to the new economy will eventually wither and possibly die out.

Understanding Free Software Licenses

Both "free" and "open source" software provide alternatives to the proprietary model. These are two similar software licensing models with one fairly subtle – but sometimes contentious – difference. The primary difference between the two models lies in whose freedom is being propagated – the users' or the developers'. In short, free software propagates the users' freedom while open source software propagates the developers' freedom. Beyond this difference, the two are synonymous.

Those who lean toward the free software model consider it necessary, in the free software license, to prevent developers from being able to restrict other people's freedom. Those who lean toward the open source model tend to uphold the developer's right to choose whether their software is proprietary or not. While the two models generally have attracted their own camps of followers, many people (Christian or not) agree that both models are preferable to the proprietary model.

Free software licenses guarantee four fundamental freedoms (the Free Software Definition http://www.gnu.org/philosophy/free-sw.html):

- Freedom to run the program for any purpose

- Freedom to study the program to see how it works

- Freedom to redistribute the program to help others

- Freedom to modify or improve the program, and to release the improvements so that the whole community may benefit.

The GNU General Public License (GPL) is the most popular free software license. It is also what is known as a "copyleft" license. The copyleft sits on top of, so to speak, the copyright, and adds a restriction that prohibits developers from placing any additional restrictions on modified versions of the software they release to the community. Thus, all versions of the software remain free. Copyleft is a tool to ensure that programs you release will always be free.

Many people think of non-copylefted free software as "open source", due to confusion over the terminology. However, "free software" and "open source" software are essentially the same. The Free Software Foundation and the Open Source Initiative use different criteria for determining whether a particular license meets their standards. The GNU General Public License is both, a "free" and an "open source" license. However, some licenses accepted by the Open Source Initiative are not compatible with the GNU GPL.

Software that is in the Public Domain is a special case of free software. It is modifiable and sharable. Like non-copylefted free software, software in the public domain can be modified and the modified version released with restrictions. The primary difference is that free software is copyrighted, whereas the public domain software is not. Thus, if someone violates the distribution terms of your free software license (whether copyleft or non-copyleft), developers can enforce the terms.

It is important to note that free software licenses (at least, those that are GPL compatible) require access to the source code. Either the source code, or a written offer for it, must accompany the binaries. One is not permitted to charge a fee for the source code that exceeds the fee charged for the binaries. In other words, a developer may charge a fee, both for downloading the binaries (or via CD), and for the source. However, the source must be "equally accessible".

The Free Software Foundation offers a great deal of information pertaining to the use of the GPL. They also have a page defining terms that are often used in misleading ways. You can find information about GPL-compatible licenses, conditions under which GPL'ed software can be used with non-free software. It is vitally important, if Christians are to grasp the differences between free and non-free software, that we understand the language and concepts involved.

The Open Source Definition is essentially the same (albeit longer) and is included, in annotated form, in the back of this book. Numerous licenses are approved by the Open Source Initiative, which uses less stringent criteria than the Free Software Foundation. For instance, the Open Source Initiative has accepted licenses that have been rejected by the Free Software Foundation as being too restrictive. Many programs included with a typical GNU/Linux distribution include one or another of the available licenses. There is a subtle difference between "free" software licenses and some "open source" licenses.

So-called "shared source" is recent reaction from certain proprietary vendors and falls woefully short of being "open", let alone "free". "Shared Source" allows external developers to view and even modify the source code. However, they still must sign non-disclosure agreements and their modifications belong to the original developer – not them or their employers. This still prohibits the freedom of the external developers to modify software for their own internal use. In most cases, source code is restricted to academic or non-commercial use. At any rate, "shared" source is not free or open source – it is too restrictive.

Freedom in Licensing

Christians need to wrestle with a few questions long and hard. Does the owner of the computer have the right to control that computer – that is, when, where, and how it is used? Do users have the right to know what is in the source code before they run the software on their computers? Do users have the right to modify the tools they use to suit their system and task requirements? Do I, as a Christian developer, have the right to force users to depend on me for modifications?

Few other tools require the kind of dependence that is built into every single proprietary software license. Technical skill, money and other issues may propel the user to a vendor who can modify or fix the tools properly, but no license prevents such modifications. Copyright law does not prevent the modification or defacement of a book or music recording by the person who purchased it, as long as it is not redistributed. Yet, proprietary software licenses prevent this kind of action, regardless of whether or not one redistributes the software.

A Peruvian congressman authored a bill that would require Peru's government agencies to use only free software. In response to the concerns of a proprietary vendor, the congressman explained his bill as follows:

"What the Bill does express clearly, is that, for software to be acceptable for the state it is not enough that it is technically capable of fulfilling a task, but that further the contractual conditions must satisfy a series of requirements regarding the license, without which the State cannot guarantee the citizen adequate processing of his data, watching over its integrity, confidentiality, and accessibility throughout time, as these are very critical aspects for its normal functioning."

- Dr. Edgar David Villanueva Nuñez (8 April 2002, English version, Open Source Initiative website http://opensource.org/docs/peru_and_ms.php).

Dr. Nuñez argues at length that, in order to guarantee a free society, citizens, many of whom work for the Peruvian government) must have access to the underlying source code to ensure the stability of the software, and to be able to modify it for their own requirements. The free access issue affects education (especially in the United States) as well. Whereas proprietary software forbids studying the source code, free software guarantees free access to the code (the information that underpins the resulting program).

A number of governments outside the United States fear that certain vendors might be working in tandem with the CIA to monitor their governments. United States citizens should know that some vendors have the ability to detect users' software settings via the Internet, as if taking a direct cue from George Orwell. A number of privacy organizations are actively promoting privacy and freedom, both on the Internet and in our civic affairs. The Free Software Foundation offers a list of these watchdog organizations on its website.

Since we have seen in this chapter a great deal of terminology and concepts that may seem quite confusing, it may be helpful to see the various freedoms granted by different licenses. It is also useful to understand how the commercial or non-commercial nature of a software distribution may impact its license. The table on the following page will make things somewhat clearer.

Rights Granted by Proprietary Licenss & FOSS Licenses						
	Use for any purpose	Study	Modify	Redis-tribute	Release Open	Release Closed
Public Domain	X	X	X	X	X	X
Commercial Proprietary	X					
Share-Ware (Proprietary)				X*		
Free-ware (Proprietary)				X		
FOSS (Copyleft)	X	X	X	X	X	
FOSS (Non-Copyleft)	X	X	X	X	X	X
* Only the un-registered copies may be redistributed.						

As one can see from the table above, the only real difference between "non-copylefted" licenses and public domain software is that FOSS is copyrighted software. The copyright does allow developers to fight violations of the distribution terms. In most cases, this has proven to be unnecessary. Copyleft licenses include a restriction that prevents a future developer from adding further restrictions to the modified version. The idea is that the software is kept "free" for every user.

Some people suggest that the developer has the right to determine how to release his software, and view the GPL as restricting the developer. In other words a "non-copyleft" license allows the developer to take code that has been released to the community as free (open) software, and make a proprietary derivative. Thus, the developer is given the right to restrict other people's freedom, even though he has benefited from that very freedom.

The Open Source Initiative (www.opensource.org) argues that it makes little sense to develop proprietary software. Even so, Apple's Mac OS X is based on FreeBSD, but is a proprietary system. There is a version of what Apple has developed, called "GNU-Darwin" that is free software. Apple, which now ranks as one of the major contributors to the open source community, should take the next step and release its code under a free/open license. This will show that they have fully grasped the philosophical underpinnings of free software.

As mentioned previously, most proprietary licenses restrict the use of a program to a single copy of the software used by the user on a single computer. Other restrictions may involve educational or non-commercial uses. For instance, many freeware programs are only free (*gratis*) for non-commercial use. Software donated to ministries and schools by Microsoft often specify that the software must only be used for "institutional purposes". FOSS licenses make no such restrictions.

It should be noted, especially for consultants who work with religious and non-profit organizations, the terms "free" and "open" do not rule out the ability to profit from your labors. Developers can write software and sell it all day long. The Free Software Foundation sells quite a bit of software – and with quite a price tag on it. Red Hat, a Raleigh, North Carolina-based company learned how to profit from free and open source software. Most organizations sell the technical expertise, which is the biggest cost associated with software anyway.

Some developers don't want their competitors to have access to their source code. The ironic thing is that, if and when the competitor enhances the software, the original developer also benefits. Both competitors benefit from expending less money in developing software, and the customer realizes a cost savings. Thus, instead of competing, the two collaborate. Essentially, it amounts to a win-win-win situation.

The nature of free and open source licenses has helped to create a very competitive software market. Rather than a single vendor with a monopoly, several vendors offer a broad range of solutions. From Linspire's family-friendly distribution, sold through Wal-Mart, to Novell and Red Hat's predominantly business-oriented solutions, users will find a vendor with solid software and services. Along with the choice of vendors and their solutions is a variety of prices.

Ironically, the charge has been made that FOSS is somehow a communist concept. One can almost picture Comrade Jones developing a new program for "the people". Some seem to imagine that developers must give up any semblance of earning an income at all. As mentioned above, FOSS has spawned new business ventures. Red Hat is an enterprise GNU/Linux vendor in Raleigh, North Carolina. SUSE AG was purchased by Novell, the networking giant. Numerous other businesses have sprung up with the rise of the FOSS community.

Many vendors distribute free and open source software also include non-free programs in their distributions, including these listed above. Many in the free software community consider this unethical and try to avoid it. Additionally, a number of businesses have proffered their own licenses under the term "open source", even though, at times, their terms are too restrictive to meet the standards of either, the Free Software Foundation or the Open Source Initiative.

It is true that many programs are not only free, as in *libre*, but also as in *gratis*, free of cost. Yet even the gratis software can be had for a price. People are becoming consultants, support technicians, documentation writers, and finding other ways to profit from FOSS. Some have found ways to profit – or raise funds, in the case of non-profits – from the sale of free software CDs.

FOSS is neither capitalist nor communist. It encourages people to build on the foundation already laid. FOSS reduces duplicitous efforts and inspires collaboration and creativity. It reduces selfishness and promotes community. It reduces development costs and improves stability. The challenge for businesses is to learn how to profit from it. The challenge for the Church is to learn how to deploy it effectively.

5. THE HARDWARE COMPATIBILITY CHALLENGE

Perhaps the most important issue is whether GNU/Linux is compatible with your current hardware. One thing you should do is to check the various GNU/Linux hardware resources to see if your hardware is compatible. Proprietary operating system vendors usually publish some sort of hardware compatibility list. There are several such resources, independent and vendor-specific, for GNU/Linux as well.

You will find a few of these in the Resources section of this book, and would be wise to investigate them. Take a bit of time to try to determine the specifications of your hardware. You will want to know the make and model number, as well as other factors, such as speed, storage space or frequency, depending on your device. At least know your make and model. If you don't see your device listed or described as functioning, you should attempt to find out if anyone else has got such a device working. Google can be your friend at this point.

GNU/Linux will run most of the common hardware out of the box these days. Hardware auto-detection varies from one GNU/Linux distribution to another, but the most popular distributions do an excellent job of auto-detecting and configuring hardware these days. Certain peripherals may or may not be supported, depending on the manufacturer. In some cases you will still have to download drivers from the Internet to get a certain device working correctly.

While the commercial GNU/Linux distributions often support the widest range of hardware, some of the newer non-commercial distributions offer strong competition in this area. Downloading drivers is really only a minor inconvenience in most cases. By comparison, most device drivers for proprietary operating systems require either the device manufacturers CD, or a download from the Internet. It is fair to say that DVD codecs are not distributed with most GNU/Linux distributions, due to legal issues, but are available as a download from the Internet.

When hardware is not supported by GNU/Linux at all, it is typically a problem of the vendor refusing to release its drivers for that product. The reasons vary, but typically, there is a misunderstanding of what the FOSS community is asking. In one case, the FOSS community simply wanted to be allowed to distribute the driver binaries with their operating system distribution. A well-designed e-mail campaign helped convince the manufacturer to release the drivers to the community.

It is important to note that, while many devices will work with GNU/Linux, you will do well to note a few observations regarding certain devices. It is also important to understand that some devices may require a bit of tweaking in order to get them working correctly. It isn't necessarily a big deal, but it might cause confusion initially. Let's consider some of the different types of hardware that could trip up some users.

I've installed several monitors with GNU/Linux without a hitch. I recommend getting to know your monitor's specifications to be safe. Most GNU/Linux installation programs offer the opportunity to test your settings before making them final. SUSE's Yast also allows you to adjust the width and height of the display frame. GNU/Linux can handle most monitors very well.

If you still rely on a dial-up modem, you may need to change yours. The typical internal modem that comes with a Windows system is not likely to work with GNU/Linux. They are software-controlled, which makes them cheaper, but also slower and OS-specific. In spite of the fact that GNU/Linux is improving support for Win-modems, you'll be better off with an external, hardware-controlled model. Although they cost a bit more, you definitely get what you pay for.

For cable/DSL connections, you'll want a router, which is where that old 486 PC comes in handy. Just toss GNU/Linux in, and convert it to a router (saves you from having to buy one). There are several distributions designed specifically for this purpose. Some can even be run from a single floppy disk. Of course, you can purchase a hardware router off the shelf. Routers are operating system independent and have the added advantage of offering decent protection from un-wanted Internet traffic.

GNU/Linux usually handles printers very well. I have a fancy HP 970 Cse, complete with duplexer attachment. Using either of the two available printing systems allows me to print decent documents. I use CUPS, as it provides the best drivers for my printer. Combined with OpenOffice.org, I'm a dangerous man.

However, some printers are notorious for poor performance – or even not working – under GNU/Linux. You really should refer to the resources in the back of the book for more information.

Most storage drives, such as Zip, Jazz, and flash storage devices work well with GNU/Linux. Most Palm devices work with GNU/Linux – many run GNU/Linux. Cameras and scanners vary. A number of MP3 players are supported as well. Whatever your device, GNU/Linux likely supports at least a couple models like it.

Unfortunately, for various reasons, vendors may not advertise their product as compatible with GNU/Linux, even if it does work. Additionally, some vendors do not seem to have much interest in opening their drivers to the open source community. This means we have to do a little homework. Again, though, in most cases, your standard hardware from major vendors should work.

6. THE INTEROPERABILITY CHALLENGE

You'll also want to know if GNU/Linux is "well-adjusted" socially – that is, whether it plays well with other operating systems and applications. It's important to know the answer to this because, in a world where people choose Windows because "that's what everyone uses", you need to know if you can connect to PC's that run other operating systems and share files between Microsoft Office on Windows and OpenOffice.org on GNU/Linux. The good news is that GNU/Linux is superbly adjusted.

Interoperability Across the Network

For starters, GNU/Linux can connect to pretty much any other operating system across a network. Various tools enable users to continue using legacy programs that run under their current system. Most of the application software available for GNU/Linux can import and export documents and data from and to Windows-based application formats. Let's look a little closer.

A system running GNU/Linux can connect to other UNIX systems, Mac (OS X is actually UNIX underneath), and Windows. Connecting computers this way in your office is what we call networking. The Local Area

Network (LAN) is what you'll use within your facility. Networking requires communications protocols that allow the computers to understand each other.

Many businesses that use Windows on the desktop workstation connect them to a GNU/Linux file and print server using SAMBA. Windows uses the SMB protocol for file and printer sharing; GNU/Linux and UNIX systems use the NFS protocol. SAMBA simply allows GNU/Linux and Windows machines to share files and printers with each other.

GNU/Linux also offers AppleTalk, the Mac networking protocol, and Novell's IPX protocol. In fact, Novell recently acquired SUSE Linux and Ximian, the maker of Ximian Evolution, the Outlook clone. Novell recently committed itself to the open source movement. Since GNU/Linux was built for multi-user, networked environments it is able to connect to other computers in a variety of ways.

This means you can run one PC with GNU/Linux while maintaining your current Windows – and other boxes – all while you adjust to the new OS. It also means you can migrate gradually if that fits your needs better. Of course, it's possible that a church could have a mixture of donated hardware. In this case, you can run GNU/Linux, Mac, and Windows without missing a beat!

Office Productivity Interoperability

Office productivity is one of the reasons why so many people try to use the same software. This book was created using both Microsoft Word under Windows XP Pro and OpenOffice.org under SUSE Linux Pro 9.2. That's proof positive that OpenOffice.org works very well with Microsoft Office. In fact, OpenOffice.org is probably more interoperable than its proprietary competitors. It is difficult to get *any* non-Microsoft software to work well with Office. Still, OpenOffice.org does the job very well.

The two formatting glitches, spacing and images in PNG format were easily fixed. I found that with spacing, I can either make the minor adjustments or ignore them altogether, knowing that when I re-open the document in OpenOffice.org I will have it exactly the way it should be. The same goes for images. For some reason, Microsoft Office did not handle the PNG images inserted into the OpenOffice.org document well at all. It does fine with PNG images inserted from within MS Office, and handles JPEG images well.

The problem with the images is one example of the problems caused by proprietary applications. Since they are poorly documented – if at all – they are nearly impossible for developers of other applications to work with. If Microsoft and other vendors opened up their proprietary formats, other applications would work much better. OpenOffice.org, on the other hand, offers a publicly available document format. This improves interoperability and opens the door to establishing a standard.

One very important aspect pertaining to interoperability is the fact that OpenOffice.org's OpenDocument format will soon be an ISO standard. This means that the format will be recognized by government entities and used by other office suites. The truth is that KOffice, Sun's StarOffice, IBM's WorkPlace (a web-based collaboration suite) and other office productivity software already support the OpenDocument format. The proprietary competitors that do not support it could leave themselves out in the cold.

Several products exist that allow users to run Windows applications, such as Microsoft Office, Quicken, and a number of others under GNU/Linux. This software typically requires a dual-boot system. Other products allow users to run the Windows operating system under GNU/Linux, and thus any applications that run on Windows. Most of the offerings in this arena are commercial, though there may be a free (gratis) version available. WINE (Wine Is Not An Emulator) is a free distribution, and is the basis of Codeweavers Crossover.

Xandros, SUSE, and other GNU/Linux vendors make use of the Code Weavers Crossover distribution to enable users to continue using their legacy Windows applications. Win4Lin allows users to run Windows 98 in a window on a GNU/Linux desktop, such as KDE. Doing some homework, including checking out reviews of these products might help to save a little heartache at the end of the day. Whereas GNU/Linux attempts to adhere to readily available open standards and with proprietary products, it is difficult to find proprietary software that adheres to open standards, and work seamlessly with other proprietary programs.

Interoperability in the office productivity arena is likely the most important issue for most church users. The biggest challenge for free and open source software developers is that most proprietary applications store documents and data in a proprietary format that is difficult to render perfectly in another program. This is one reason why many people are dropping proprietary applications – it's easier to extract data from and exchange data with the open source solutions.

OpenOffice.org is the best office suite available when it comes to compatibility with Microsoft Office. Its Word equivalent, Writer, works best of all. Calc works very well with Excel spreadsheets. Impress has had a history of not working quite as well with PowerPoint, but simple presentations will work. Until recently (Base will be part of the 2.0 release), there has been no Access replacement. However, OpenOffice.org enables users to connect directly to any ODBC- or JDBC-compliant database.

You may need to make some minor adjustments to your documents as you open them in each OpenOffice.org program. For instance, you may discover your page breaks don't work out quite the same. Often – simply by placing the cursor in an innocuous blank line, and hitting the [Backspace] – you'll be fine. The image on the cover of this document seemed to keep getting goofed, as it's really two images. I fixed it in OOo, only to find it re-goofed in Word. I left it alone in Word, and discovered it was still fine back in OOo.

Between Excel and OOo, you may or may not need to readjust the cell alignment when you open your files. Again, it is no big deal. Between PowerPoint and OOo, you may lose some functionality, which would be true if switching between PowerPoint 97 and PowerPoint 2000. These are issues that arise anytime people use different applications and platforms. They are not debilitating, and certainly a non-issue for a typical church.

GnuCash imports Quicken files, including bank records, which utilize the Quicken format. MyBooks is a commercial financial accounting distribution that also works with Quicken and QuickBooks. Ultimately, most users will discover that free and open source software tends to be highly interoperable with proprietary software.

7. THE USABILITY CHALLENGE

Whether GNU/Linux is easier or more difficult to use than other systems is, to me, a matter of perspective. If you're using GNU/Linux as a desktop workstation, it isn't necessarily more difficult to use than the others. It *is* different. Different is not necessarily more difficult. You get more choices with GNU/Linux, which adds to the fear one may feel when faced with several desktops to choose from at the login prompt. Even so, usability is a fair issue to address.

Allow me to share the story of a 55-year-old lady who uses Mandrake Linux. She produces various homemade craft items and shares photos of her work with her fellow crafters across the Internet, a predominantly female crowd. After having suffered a number of viruses with her legacy software, she was encouraged to try GNU/Linux. After spending some time investigating GNU/Linux thoroughly, she settled on Mandrake Linux.

This non-technical user then managed to install her own firewall, choosing to install one she chose, rather than accepting the default firewall system included with Mandrake Linux. It took her a little time, and one can be certain she relied on help from e-mail lists. If a middle-aged lady without a background in computer technology can manage to switch to GNU/Linux, and install her own firewall, there is absolutely no reason to

---

suggest that GNU/Linux is "too difficult" for "non-techies".

Setting Up Hardware

When I bought my HP 970 Cse to print with Windows 98, I had to jump through hoops backwards to install it. I missed a step somewhere along the way, and even the vendor's tech support couldn't help me un-install the driver correctly. I ended up formatting the hard drive and reinstalling the OS just to get the printer installed. Talk about frustrating!

When I upgraded from Windows 98 to Windows XP Professional, I decided to start with a clean installation. After formatting the hard drive, and installing XP, I then attempted to reinstall my CD burning software that came with my CD-Writer. Naturally, the CD burning software's installation program was time-limited. I was prevented from being able to write CDs in Windows unless I upgraded. Browsing to the vendor's web site, I discovered that the upgrade was a whopping $70.00!

Many people I know – experienced Windows technicians included – experienced recurring nightmares from having installed so-called "plug-n-play" modems. The night operator at one corporate office has to reboot some of the Windows servers every morning before he leaves. There are numerous horror stories, and you may have a few of your own. All I am saying is that even the so-called "easy-to-use" systems offer challenges. When taken in perspective, one might be hard pressed to say one system is easier than another.

Usable Command-Line

Some people seem to think that GNU/Linux only offers a command-line interface – a scary prospect for many. But it also has several graphical interfaces. You won't be forced to stare at command prompts all day. The important issue is that GNU/Linux has kept the graphical shells separate from the underlying operating system, thus making it more stable. We have to bear in mind that the command-line interface does offer some distinct advantages.

Many people fear command-line interfaces, considering them old and arcane. When I think back to my early experiences with DOS 6.22, it's not difficult to imagine why. If you realized at the end of a long command that you goofed back near the beginning, you had to retype most of the command. With GNU/Linux, you can edit the command where it needs to be edited. Although I prefer the graphical interfaces, the GNU/Linux command line is a joy to use.

In fact, the GNU/Linux command line offers a history function, the settings for which you can adjust to your liking. This comes in handy if you happen to be using the command line to run a particular command several times. I frequently use the command line for interacting with the MySQL database server. In doing so, I can simply hit the "Up" arrow key to bring up the last command. I can then edit it to login as a different user – or make other changes – and re-run the command.

Usable Graphical Desktops

In some respects, GNU/Linux offers more intuitive graphical shells than Windows. The desktop known as Enlightenment eliminates the task bar in favor of simply clicking or right-clicking on the desktop. The focus is on efficiency – just click on the desktop, and there's your "start" button. Most graphical shells offer a concept called "virtual desktops" which allow users to organize their work in a more intuitive fashion. For instance, think of having one desk for your office tasks, and another for your Internet-related tasks.

As far as graphical shells (desktops) are concerned, three are probably the easiest to use in a typical church environment. It is possible to install all of them on a given system, and then choose which one to load at the login prompt. However, this may not be suitable for your system, especially if you have limited hardware resources. The needs and tastes of your administrator and/or users will dictate which you need to use.

The fact that the graphical shells are separate from the underlying operating system makes it easier to offer users a choice between several shells. The graphical shells basically take different approaches to managing applications and windows. As we look at these graphical shells briefly, you should know that most applications run on all of the various shells, and that just because an application is designed for KDE, doesn't necessarily mean it won't run under GNOME or another desktop.

One difference users will have to adjust to is the idea of mounting and un-mounting removable media.

Floppy disks, CDs and USB devices all need to be mounted manually. This is automatically handled by Windows, but is very much a manual process in GNU/Linux. Ordinarily, you can simply click on a pre-defined icon on your desktop by right-clicking on the desktop to see them listed in the context menu. Still, it does take some getting used to.

KDE, one of the most common desktops in use, is the most like Microsoft Windows in its look and feel. Users will find the system menu ("Start" button) in the same place – the lower left corner of the screen. There's a launch bar to launch commonly-used applications. The task bar shows what windows are open. The system tray shows processes running in the background.

For the most part, icons and windows behave much the same way as in Windows. One difference is that the applications installed show up in pre-arranged categories in the system menu. Many Windows users manually setup categories of software in the start menu. With GNU/Linux, this is an automated process, making applications easy to find based on what they do. Additionally, windows can be "rolled up" by double-clicking on the title bar.

GNOME is another popular desktop, which is generally considered to be light-weight, meaning that it consumes fewer system resources than KDE. GNOME still functions similar to Windows, but the system menu now is usually found at the top-left corner of the screen. This is not always true – different distributions setup their graphical shells differently. It offers many of the same features as KDE, but does not include quite as many applications.

Illustration 6 - The GNOME desktop (SUSE Linux 9.2)

The GNOME desktop (Illus. 6) has the main panel at the top of the screen, and the task bar at the bottom. The task bar in Windows can be placed at the top as well. The main panel shows a few icons added for quick starting of commonly-used programs. Icons on the desktop let you access your CD and other media easily. Users can easily add and remove quick start icons to and from the main panel by right-clicking and using the context menu.

XFce is the true light-weight desktop, offering few of the features of KDE or GNOME, and consuming the fewest resources. A simple panel across the bottom offers some "launchers" or menus (depending on what you set up). The background and desktop theme can be changed, along with a few other items. This is a great desktop for administrators to deploy with the non-technical users.

An administrator can easily setup the applications a user will need, and then show the user which icons launch which applications. This setup (Illus. 7, below) is probably fairly typical, consisting mostly of application launchers on the left, the virtual desktop pager in the middle, and system launchers on the right. The OpenOffice.org applications are accessible from the OpenOffice.org launcher.

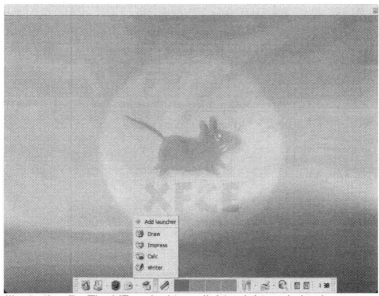

Illustration 7 - The XFce desktop - lightweight and simple

Creating launchers (setting up your icons that launch programs) in XFce is very simple. Right-clicking on the main panel brings up a context menu, from which you can choose to setup a launcher. In the ensuing dialog box you can enter the command (or browse for it), and pick an icon to match. In most cases, the command is the same as the program name – i.e., Firefox = firefox.

KDE makes the most sense when you want your users to have an environment most like Windows. Use GNOME when you want a light-weight desktop, but want to still offer your users a fair amount of control over their desktops. XFce makes the most sense when you have a bunch of non-technical users, or if you have limited hardware resources.

There are additional desktops that can be used. Some eliminate the task bar in favor of simply clicking on the desktop to bring up the system menu. The idea is that wherever your mouse is on the desktop, you can click and have the system menu at your pleasure. It's a very efficient approach. You may want evaluate them to see if they fit your needs.

Usability of Productivity Applications

When it comes to office productivity, most of the concepts are the same. In fact, many of the toolbar icons in OpenOffice.org are the same as in Microsoft Office. The tool-tips will help with many of the differences. Again, though, different is not more difficult. OpenOffice.org 2.0 will look more like Microsoft Office, but allows users to retain the old look & feel as well.

Perhaps the Gimp (a PhotoShop-like image editor) is the one program that seems to be quite different in its user interface. Even so, most of the folks I know that have used both prefer the Gimp. Apparently, even the Gimp is susceptible to getting the imitation look and feel. The new version will look more like Adobe's Photoshop.

OpenOffice.org offers an auto-complete feature – and not just dates. Once you type a word in a new document, you need only type the first few letters of that same word again to bring up the rest of the word. If that's the word you want, just hit the Enter key and keep moving. If you're typing a similar word, just keep typing until it pops up. I wonder how much time I saved using OOo to type much of this document?

There are some subtle differences between OpenOffice.org and Microsoft Office that may not be immediately apparent to some users. In Microsoft Office, users generally define "sections" to change the page layout between, say, the front matter and the content of a book. Users define "page styles" in OpenOffice.org. It's very similar to formatting a paragraph.

OpenOffice.org 2.0 includes an Access-like database feature that may just go a step further than Microsoft Access. The OpenOffice.org database application takes advantage of the World Wide Web Consortium's XForm standard for web-based data entry, which will eventually replace the current HTML forms used in so many web pages. However, OOo 2.0 is a much more powerful XForms client than the currently existing clients.

OpenOffice.org 2.0 adds new chart types and also improves interoperability with Microsoft Office tremendously. Impress is better able to deal with comments in a PowerPoint file. It also offers an interface more like PowerPoint. The sorting feature in Calc has been changed to behave more like the sorting feature in Excel. Many other improvements have been made as well.

Mozilla's Firefox web browser functions similarly to Internet Explorer. However, its tabbed browsing feature reduces the number of windows users have open at once. Tabbed browsing technology has been around since the days of Windows 3.11, yet Microsoft has failed to implement it. Firefox is extensible through easily developed extensions, like the Super Bible Toolbar, that allows users to search The Bible Gateway right from within Firefox. The extensions are available through the Mozilla website.

GnuCash is similar to Quicken. It isn't quite as fancy, but works for personal and business finances. Where Quicken uses categories, GnuCash uses double-entry accounting. Learning to split transactions is a little tricky at first. However, once you get the hang of it, you'll be o.k. If you're familiar at all with Quicken, you should be able to manage the change just fine.

The Sword Projects - BibleTime, GnomeSword, Bible Desktop, and MacSword – generally use interfaces similar to the On-Line Bible for Windows. Selecting books, chapters and verses uses a similar approach, allowing the user to select each in succession. Adding bible and reference modules is a simple matter of opening the module management dialog and selecting the modules you want.

While there are numerous educational applications for Windows, the selection for GNU/Linux systems is significantly smaller. These applications are the least likely to look like their Windows-based counterparts. That said, the applications available are very interesting and often pretty innovative. KTouch and Tux are two typing tutors that work very well, and are aimed as much at children as adults.

KDE and GNOME include a number of educational programs that span a broad range of knowledge - Geometry, astronomy, languages, and even programming. GCompris is a general skills builder for children aged 2-10 that makes use of "story boards". Keduca allows parents and teachers, including Bible teachers, to make up quizzes for students. Most of the programs available for education are well-designed and provide a level of sophistication not seen in many proprietary packages.

Multimedia is an area where GNU/Linux can excel. The familiar Real Player program runs on GNU/Linux. Audacity is used to record worship services and other audio tracks in a number of churches. Broadcast 2000 and Main Actor let folks produce high-quality video clips. XMMS is a theme-able CD/MP3 player similar to WinAmp. And yes, you can watch T.V. with one of several GNU/Linux applications on your T.V. tuner card.

Usability of System Management Tools

Some of the installation, configuration, and maintenance tasks might pose more of a challenge, especially to non-technical users. Even so, in many cases, the real difficulty lies in the unwillingness to adapt to the new system. If you understand the various network services, and can configure them in Windows, all you need in GNU/Linux is to find the right tools, and the rest should be easy.

Instead of the System Console, with its snap-ins and add-ons, you'll have to get used to using different tools. For instance, SUSE uses a tool called, *Yast (Yet Another Setup Tool)* to accomplish most tasks. Red Hat and Mandrake offer different tools that accomplish the same things. These tools allow administrators to manage their hardware, software, networking, and users from a single interface.

A major advantage is that, instead of wrestling with the Registry (where you can never be sure you completely eliminated a driver or other tidbit), you can edit a text file directly to make changes, if necessary. Because I was unable to completely remove the HP printer driver from the Windows 98 Registry, I had to completely re-install the system. Even Reg Cleaner didn't help.

With DOS and Windows 3.11, users and administrators could edit a file to adjust settings or correct the minor piece of information that got missed during cleanup. So, too, with GNU/Linux systems, administrators can do exactly that. What a blessing to be able to edit a file and move on to the next task!

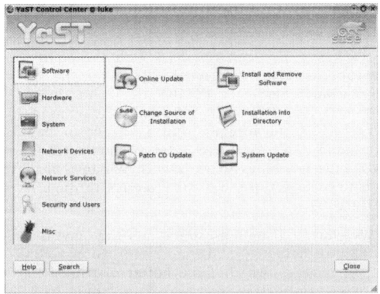

Illustration 8 - SUSE's Yast eases system management tasks

The image above shows Yast, Novell/SUSE's system configuration tool. Users can install RPM packages via standard console commands, using a graphical RPM tool, or Yast. Yast maintains a database of your RPMs, and you can tell Yast where to find RPMs not on the installation media. Yast On-Line Update (YOU) keeps your system up to date with the latest security patches and bug fixes.

Webmin is another system administration tool available. It runs in a web browser, and works with pretty much any of the GNU/Linux systems. Because it uses a web interface, it is relatively easy to use. The CUPS printing system (the most popular of two such systems) also has a web interface by which it can be managed. For those who need to, the text files in /etc are much easier to manage than the Windows Registry.

When it comes to file and print services, Windows uses the SMB protocol. GNU/Linux uses the Network filesystem (NFS). Frankly, it's pretty easy to setup using SUSE's Yast. You can run NFS with the Light-weight Directory Assistance Protocol (LDAP) or the Network Information Service (NIS) to centralize user administration. NIS is older, but still widely used. LDAP offers certain advantages, and is likely to be better understood by Windows administrators. To setup GNU/Linux machines to work with Windows machines, you'll need to setup the Samba service through its web interface.

We have dispelled some of the myths about GNU/Linux being "too difficult" for "non-techies" to use. We have shown that the better distributions offer graphical administration tools. You should have some idea that a GNU/Linux-based graphical desktop is just as easy to use as Windows, as are most applications. Before we address the costs involved with migrating to GNU/Linux, you may wish to have a list of applications that would replace your current legacy software.

The tables on the following pages show the GNU/Linux equivalents to the well-known Windows applications you use every day. You'll find a column for the task, then a column each for the applications that run on GNU/Linux (and BSD) and Windows. The applications listed that run on GNU/Linux are simply the most popular and best known. Additionally, Firefox, Thunderbird, and OpenOffice.org, among others – also run on Windows.

Task	Windows	GNU/BSD
Office Suites	MS Office	OpenOffice.org
	WordPerfect	Koffice
		Siag
Word Processing	MS Word	OOo Writer
		KWrite
		AbiWord
Spreadsheet	MS Excel	OOo Calc
		Kspread
Presentation	MS PowerPoint	OOo Impress
		KPresent
Database	MS Access	OOo Base
Desktop Publishing	MS Publisher	OOo Writer
		Scribus
Image Editing	MS Draw	OOo Draw
Project Management	MS Project	Mr. Project
Text Editing	NotePad	EMACS
(System files)	Context	VIM
	jEdit	jEdit
	VIM	Kate/gedit
File Management	Windows Explorer	Konqueror
		Nautilus
		Midnight Commander
Church Management	ACS	InfoCentral
	Power Church	CHADDB
	Servant Keeper	
Financial Management	Quicken	GnuCash
	QuickBooks	MyBooks*
	PeachTree Accounting	

*Commercial

The Usability Challenge

Task	Windows	GNU/BSD
E-Mail	Outlook Outlook Express Thunderbird	Evolution Sylpheed-Claws Thunderbird
Web Browsing	Internet Explorer Mozilla/Firefox Netscape Opera	Konqueror Mozilla/Firefox Netscape Opera
Image/Photo editing	PhotoShop Paint Shop Pro	The Gimp OOo Draw
Database Servers	MS SQL Oracle MySQL	MySQL PostGreSQL Oracle
Educational	Kaplan	GCompris Keduca Mathematica KTouch (typing tutor) XPlanet
Multimedia	Windows Player Real Player	Real Player XMMS
CD Burning	Nero Roxio	K3B X CD Roast
Audio Production	Audacity	Audacity Rosegarden

8. THE COST CHALLENGE

Have you given much thought to the cost of computing? Have you pondered the possibility that your present computing platform could actually represent poor stewardship of your church's resources? Cost is not the only factor in your decision, and not even necessarily the most important. Yet, if you could reasonably manage your church for less money than you currently do, wouldn't you want to explore that option further? You might be able to help one more family, or boost a missionary's efforts, purchase new bibles, or a number of things.

While hardware costs have dropped significantly over time, software costs are increasing significantly. It used to be that you would pay $1300 for the hardware and less than $100 for the operating system. Now the operating system costs nearly as much as the hardware and the application software is often astronomical. This makes absolutely no sense given that the cost of distributing software is a far cry from the cost of distributing computer hardware.

There are a number of factors pertaining to cost. Church leaders need to consider the potential need to retrain the staff. Migrating your ministry's data will prove to be a tedious task, but certainly not an impossible one. GNU/Linux may not work with some of a ministry's hardware, but may extend the life of other hardware. A good strategy based on your ministry's situation can make the migration path smoother, and generally reduces the upfront costs involved with an overnight approach.

There is another factor to consider as you calculate your migration costs. The cost of future upgrades should be taken into account. The initial cost of migrating to new software might be higher than the cost of simply upgrading. However, once you migrate to free and open source software the future costs are much, much lower than that of the proprietary vendors. It is also much easier to change vendors if you begin to experience problems with your current vendor. Let's look at an example of this.

Since OpenOffice.org runs on Windows, let's take a look at the cost of migrating from Microsoft Office to OpenOffice.org. OpenOffice.org typically requires about two weeks to get used to without any retraining at all. The reason is that most of the features that are different between the two are unused by the majority of users. Most folks could easily pick right up and keep going. We'll use this as our example.

The table below shows two churches, each with five staff members. Both run some version of Microsoft Windows. One is migrating to Microsoft Office Small Business 2003 from the previous version, while the other is migrating from their current office suite to OpenOffice.org 2.0. If one assumes no productivity during the two-week transition (at a rate of $15/hour per employee), the cost of migrating is obviously higher than the cost of upgrading to the next version of the current office suite.

However, the cost of migrating to OpenOffice.org 2.0 is reduced by the fact that some productive work will be accomplished during that time. In fact, users may lose no more than a couple of hours of productivity per week during the transition period. After that, they will be back up to full productivity. Even at a loss of 25% productivity (100 man hours over the two week period), the cost is $1500.

Church A	Cost	Church B	Cost
MS Office SB 2003 (Upgrade)	$1395	OpenOffice.org 2.0	$0
MS Office SB 2003 (Full)	$2250	0% Production	$6000
97% Production	$180	90% Production	$600
		75% Production	$1500
Next Upgrade			
MS Office SB 200x (Upgrade)	$1395	OpenOffice.org	$0
97% Production	$180	97% Production	$180

The upgrade *might* be cheaper short term, but not necessarily. In the long term, however, OpenOffice.org will still be $0.00, and by the next version, users will be more than comfortable with it. Meanwhile, your organization will again have to pay out hundreds or thousands of dollars for the next proprietary upgrade.

The scenario above only involves an office suite. The differences in cost could become even more dramatic when applied to a total platform migration scenario. The difference is that some ministries will have the ability to migrate themselves, while others will feel the need to either rely on consultants or send their in-house folks for training. Alternatively, churches may be able to get help through a local Linux Users Group or The Freely Project. All of these issues should be factored into the cost of the migration.

It should be noted that this scenario is not necessarily an accurate guage. One has to account for the time spent installing and configuring the software, as well as running Microsoft Office Update. While this would not be a big deal for a church with cable or DSL, a church with a dial-up connection could spend a significant amount of time downloading the update software. There are also a number of Outlook-related security vulnerabilities that may need attending.

Installing and configuring OpenOffice.org is no more time consuming than installing Microsoft Office, and may be even less time consuming. Most people do not take advantage of the features that differ between OpenOffice.org and Microsoft Office. A good two-hour overview should get most users going, and probably would increase production during the two-week adjustment period. You may want to let your "power users" get some additional training on the more advanced tools.

We mentioned being able to switch vendors, if need be. In fact, one of the surest signs that your ministry needs to migrate is when migration costs a great deal more than upgrading. With Windows, there is only one vendor – Microsoft. The dozens of GNU/Linux vendors must compete in a stiff race for your business. Mind you, Red Hat administrators might need a little time to adapt to SUSE's Yast, but overall, your users will see pretty much the same desktop tools they've been using. In other words, once you migrate from Windows to any GNU/Linux distribution, you can migrate to any other distribution you want without further re-learning.

Migrating your data from one GNU/Linux distribution to another is merely a matter of copying it to the new system. OpenOffice.org running on Fedora Core is pretty much the same as OpenOffice.org running on SUSE Linux. So it is with other applications. Even changing desktop environments is not such a big challenge, as the core system remains the same.

If Novell starts slipping in their service or the quality of their SUSE Linux distribution, your ministry has plenty of options available. Red Hat's Fedora Core is the de facto standard in the United States. Mandrake, Xandros, and Linspire provide additional alternatives – and there are others besides. Unfortunately, proprietary software makes migration a much more difficult and costly challenge than it needs to be. This leads to what many refer to as "vendor lock-in".

Organizations experience vendor lock-in when they become trapped in a forced upgrade cycle. Typically, they need bug fixes, security patches, technical support, or new software that is unsupported on their current software. The answer from the software vendor is to upgrade. Also, some vendors distribute software that requires an upgrade after a certain period of time.

Hardware Costs

Hardware should not impact costs much at all – most common devices already work well. Once you've checked to ensure your current hardware will work with GNU/Linux, and made any necessary adjustments for hardware that may need to be replaced, then you can take it from there. In most cases, GNU/Linux would improve a computer's life, as mentioned previously. Printers and wireless network cards will need to be examined most closely.

One simple solution here is to upgrade the software when you purchase new hardware. At that point, you can choose hardware that you know will work well with GNU/Linux. If you upgrade hardware on a piecemeal basis, the GNU/Linux system can work with any current Windows systems until you upgrade the rest. A good opportunity would be to purchase a computer with Linspire from a retailer like Wal-Mart. In short, the need to purchase new hardware is minimal.

One point related to hardware is that because GNU/Linux is often available for free (gratis), ministries could purchase more and/or better hardware than they could if they chose to use expensive, proprietary software. For instance, a ministry could purchase two computers instead of one. Or the ministry could purchase a computer with a faster processor, more memory, and a bigger hard drive than it otherwise might because it does not have to count in the additional cost of software.

Upgrade Windows or Move to GNU/Linux?

What will it cost to change? Studies suggest that GNU/Linux is ideal for new organizations and those without a heavy investment in Windows-based solutions. The cost of change varies, although the larger the organization, the greater the complexity of their infrastructure, and thus, the greater the cost of change. However, that would be true if an organization migrates from GNU/Linux to Windows. Even so, many users actually suggest that their migration costs have been minimal.

The tables below show two churches, each with a staff of five persons. One is upgrading from Windows 98 to Windows XP Professional. The Windows church is merely upgrading all of its software. The other has chosen to migrate from Windows 98 to SUSE Linux 9.2 Professional. We're assuming a single cost for the church management and lyrics display software, as well as for the music typesetting software.

Windows	Upgrade	Windows	Full
Windows XP Pro	$950.00	Windows XP Pro	$1,400.00
Office SB 2003	$1,395.00	Office SB 2003	$2,250.00
Easy Worship	$428.00	Easy Worship	$428.00
PowerChurch	$139.00	PowerChurch	$595.00
Finale	$109.00	Finale	$109.00
Total	*$3,021.00*	*Total*	*$4,782.00*

An alternative approach taken by many churches is to use Microsoft Office Professional (which includes Access), and QuickBooks as their financial management software. Access is probably ok for smaller churches (as far as proprietary software goes). While it eliminates the cost of the church management software, the cost of including Access could be higher, especially when you consider multiple copies. In this case the financial comparison would look more like the table on the next page.

Windows	Upgrade	Windows	Full
Windows XP Pro	$950.00	Windows XP Pro	$1,400.00
Office Pro 2003	$1,645.00	Office SB 2003	$2,250.00
QuickBooks Pro	$600.00	QuickBooks Pro	$750.00
Easy Worship	$428.00	Easy Worship	$428.00
Finale	$109.00	Finale	$109.00
Total	*$3,732.00*	*Total*	*$4,937.00*

The additional cost of the Professional edition of Microsoft Office (Small Business edition does not include Access), plus the cost of QuickBooks, raises the bar even higher. Appgen's MyBooks (commercial software) offers a 10-user license for only $800 – a mere $50 more than the 5-user license for QuickBooks Professional. A single-user MyBooks license is a mere $60. For those interested, MyBooks runs on Windows and Mac systems as well as on GNU/Linux.

A completely free alternative to MyBooks for GNU/Linux Systems is GnuCash. GnuCash includes a payroll function and accounts are fully customizable. It is somewhat similar to Quicken/QuickBooks, albeit with a much simpler interface. Users can import financial data from the bank in Quicken format directly to GnuCash.

Most GNU/Linux distributions include thousands of programs, ranging from office to education to multimedia – shall I go on? Even if you paid the same price for GNU/linux that you paid for all the software in the above tables, you still get a huge quantity of software that still doesn't come with Windows.

GNU/Linux	Upgrade	GNU/Linux	Full
SUSE Linux 9.3	$60 ($300)	SUSE Linux 9.3	$100 ($500)
OpenOffice.org	$0	OpenOffice.org	$0
GnuCash	$0.00	GnuCash	$0.00
Lyricue	$0	Lyricue	$0
InfoCentral	$0	InfoCentral	$0
LilyPond	$0	LilyPond	$0
Total	*$60 ($300)*	*Total*	*$100 ($500)*

The table above shows a per-copy price in parentheses. Legally speaking, a church could deploy SUSE Linux at the cost of a single copy. I would encourage organizations with the financial means to purchase a copy for each system in the organization. Doing so supports the developers who have put so much effort into the software, and makes it available to those people and organizations that do not have the means. If you use a non-profit distribution, you should consider making a contribution to that organization. Even paying on a per-copy basis, churches can save a phenomenal amount of money.

The upgrade for SUSE Linux contains the full SUSE Linux system, but excludes the manuals. The logic behind this approach is that you already know the tools, thus no need for the manuals. Some people choose the full edition just to get the newer manuals. It's your choice. You should note that the cost of some

GNU/Linux distributions is absolutely free. In that case, th cost of migrating, strictly from a software perspective, is $0.00.

As an alternative, consider the Xandros Business Desktop. For less than $500, you can run GNU/Linux on five computers, and even continue using Microsoft Office – along with other programs you might use. It works with Windows NT primary domain controllers (PDC) and Windows 2000 Active Directory domains. It also includes Sun's StarOffice, the commercial (and non-free) equivalent to OpenOffice.org. Of course, churches could use the Open Circulation Edition for next to nothing.

You should realize by now that the cost of computing in the Windows environment is pretty high. Again, though, the above scenario does not account for a number of factors. The cost of Anti-virus, anti-adware, anti-spyware, and any Internet filtering software your church may deploy adds up. While there is very little need to worry about this with GNU/Linux, generally speaking, the software available is, of course, mostly free.

If your church is 501(c)(3), you may qualify for discounts on proprietary software. Many churches, though have chosen not to file for that special status, and thus don't qualify for the discounts. That means they get to pay full price, even though they are non-profit organizations by default. The upshot of it all is that many smaller churches don't have the income to get started with computers.

This puts many churches in the position of the church I mentioned at the beginning of this book –

dancing the EULA jig. From a legal standpoint, a church could be violating copyright laws and not even realize it. Things are changing, and the Windows installation program knows if it's been installed before. It won't let you install to more than one computer.

Companies have every right to enforce their copyright protection. After all, when you clicked the "I Agree" button as you installed the software, you legally bound yourself to not passing along copies of the software. Doing so in light of the typical proprietary End-User License Agreement is a matter of breaking your agreement and violating the law. As a pastor, I discourage using software illegally. Doing so destroys the church's witness to the community. That's why free and open source software is like a ram in the bush.

GNU/Linux is very different in this respect. The operating system is freely available and can legally be shared with others. In fact, sharing free and open source software is encouraged. Thus, your church can save money, and share with the local community to boot. It is important to grasp this. Now any church can help folks in the local community where technology is concerned.

GNU/Linux is distributed by numerous groups, both commercial and non-profit. This choice helps to ensure competitive pricing among the commercial versions. When it comes to choosing a distribution, you should consider the fact that the commercial vendors actually offer telephone technical support. They also make installing GNU/Linux much easier than it might otherwise be. For instance, I wouldn't recommend installing Debian GNU/Linux until you've played around with other GNU/Linux distributions for a while.

The price of GNU/Linux distributions can vary greatly, and can generally be purchased in "home" or "personal" editions, or in "professional" editions, that include a bigger selection of software. Mandrake and SUSE both offer small business solutions, and thus are solid candidates for churches of all sizes. Xandros offers a solid selection with a broad range of prices as well. Linspire is relatively cheap, and can be used with Juno's free Internet service.

Red Hat's Fedora Core distribution is essentially cost-free. Their business distribution could cost nearly $1300 to setup a server and five workstations. You could deploy SUSE's enterprise solution (server and five workstations) for roughly $1000. Frankly, SUSE Linux Professional edition, Mandrake and Xandros Desktop, with offerings in the $20-$200 range, appear to offer the best options for most churches. The advantage of the non-commercial distributions is that you can use one copy for your whole office. In other words, that's roughly $80 for all the PC's in your church office – not per PC.

Of course, if you've got a brave soul in your midst, you could order Debian CDs for about $15 (no manual with that), or download it via your broadband Internet connection. Again, shop around. In most cases, even the most expensive GNU/Linux solution would cost less than the Microsoft operating systems and their respective applications. Bear in mind that GNU/Linux includes a vast selection of application software. Whether you download GNU/Linux for free, or buy a commercial distribution, you still get to choose from hundreds of applications.

So, as far as pricing is concerned, our fledgling congregation *could have* the capability to broadcast our worship service on the Internet for about $15 (or less) for the OS, plus the cost of a video camera and a broadband connection. What's more, for that same $15 or less, we can have our choice of office suites, the best of which is OpenOffice.org, our choice of multimedia and Internet tools, even our choice of graphical desktops!

All of the free and open source church management software is currently cost-free. Perhaps the major cost will lie in extracting the data from your current application and importing it into the new database. This process of migrating your data is mostly a tedious process, and will likely consume a bit of time. However, once migrated, you will no longer be caught in the proprietary trap that keeps so many paying such huge fees for software.

Please note that the tables used for the cost analysis did not account for the cost of anti-spam, anti-virus, and anti-spyware utilities. And, for every educational application you need, say for Bible study or after school programs, you'll have to purchase a license for each copy used. Count up the cost and you'll begin to realize how the cost of proprietary software impacts the cost of computing in your organization.

Installation and Configuration Time

The time it takes to install and configure software should be considered in the equation. With proprietary platforms users purchase a basic operating system with minimal utilities and no other software included. In order to have a productive workstation, additional software usually must be purchased and installed separately. Barring the ability to copy the hard drive images to multiple hard drives, the time required simply depends on the software involved.

The typical GNU/Linux distribution already includes the vast majority of the software you need, including the office productivity software. Performing the CD shuffle to install CD burning software, office productivity software, audio recording software, and so on is reduced dramatically. It's all included with GNU/Linux. Thus, setting up a GNU/Linux workstation comparable to the typical proprietary system probably takes less time. However, because you can add so much more software, setting up GNU/Linux could take more time.

I installed SUSE Linux 9.2 during a football game one Saturday afternoon. I got the installation started, and went off and watched the game, checking on it from time to time. I installed five gigabytes of software (out of seven gigabytes) on my PC that day, and the game was just about over when the process finished. Of course, that is not a typical setup for a business environment. I made a lot of custom choices which impacted the time involved. This should give an idea of the amount of software available for GNU/Linux.

In another case, I installed the Ubuntu distribution on an old machine, running a Pentium II 450MHz processor, in just over an hour. It connects to my SUSE network just fine. It's only a single CD, but still has OpenOffice.org and Firefox. It's an extremely easy distribution to use. Be aware that root access is disabled by default, with most system tasks being performed via a special command (sudo, for those interested). Just enter your user password to gain access to the commands.

Most standard GNU/Linux installations can be completed in one or two hours, including the application software. Some installations take less time than that. Most proprietary operating systems do not include the additional software. Like the toy ads say, "all other accessories sold separately". After purchasing all the additional software, you have to install it, which generally takes 30 minutes to an hour per program. For those system administrators not familiar with GNU/Linux, a bit more time will be required to set things up initially. Even so, assuming you've done your homework, you'll save time in the long run.

The nice thing about most general-purpose GNU/Linux distributions is that they pre-configure most of the software so that it runs the way it's supposed to right out of the box. You can always tweak the settings, but most people can probably use the standard settings. For example, MySQL, a popular database server, is normally ready to run right out of the box with SUSE Linux, assuming you chose to install it with the operating system. All you have to do is use the Run-Level Editor in Yast to start it. Most proprietary operating systems require users to configure everything from scratch.

With proprietary operating systems, servers like this have to be installed and configured manually. Free and open source operating systems have the applications and servers you choose at install time ready to roll, for the most part. Some software depends on your specific system configuration, and therefore has to be configured by you to run correctly. Otherwise, the software you select during the installation process is installed and pre-configured.

You don't have to install everything at once, but it can save a good deal of time in the long run. The only reason not to is if you're not sure you're going to run the software, or you want to install and configure it your way. Oakdale Christian Fellowship has six computers networked together. Basic installations were performed on five of the computers. After that, the time it took to setup the IP addresses manually was all it took to configure the network settings. Remote desktop sharing was ready to use. File sharing was a simple routine setup.

The time spent maintaining your systems is another factor. Fighting viruses, rooting out spyware and dealing with inexplicable system crashes consumes time. In most cases, however, GNU/Linux administrators will be able to focus their efforts elsewhere, after spending a brief period configuring the security software. A thorough check of the system logs, say a couple of times a week should go a long ways toward maintaining a secure computing environment.

Some distributions include tools to automate security updates, and these are fairly easy to use.

Do It Yourself, or Get A Consultant?

Whether to go it alone or hire a consultant to help you migrate is a matter only you can decide. It depends on your ministry. If you have an in-house tech ministry, by all means, have them study the issues and lead the migration. If you have folks who are not professionals, but are knowledgeable enthusiasts, encourage them to try GNU/Linux and lead you through. If your whole congregation thinks that hitting the wrong key will blow up a computer, you might want the consultant.

If you consider consultants, make sure their plan will actually cost less than doing it yourself. Ensure they have real, hands-on experience with GNU/Linux, and check their references. A skilled consultant could save you time and money, and should be required to pass on their knowledge to your staff. Additionally, make sure you obtain some post-migration support. You may want anywhere from thirty to ninety days, depending on your comfort level.

If you decide to pay a tech guy, specify a free distribution, such as Debian (which is also highly respected), and you likely won't spend any more to migrate to GNU/Linux than you would to upgrade Windows. Even so, once you're running GNU/Linux, you'll be able to upgrade it at a fraction of the cost. I'm certain you'll miss having to pay over $200 to get a word processor that thinks it knows more about what you're doing than you do.

Pricing Resources

MS Office (Small Business Edition – includes Publisher)

http://www.officemax.com/max/solutions/product/prodBlock.jsp?
BV_UseBVCookie=yes&expansionOID=-
536907354&prodBlockOID=537141049

Easy Worship

http://www.easyworship.com/

Novell's SUSE Linux

http://www.digitalriver.com/dr/v2/ec_dynamic.main?cat_id=1&pn
=7&sid=27477

QuickBooks

http://www.officemax.com/max/solutions/search/search.jsp?bvc=
yes&searchType=product&searchString=quickbooks&searchBtn.x=
0&searchBtn.y=0

9. SYSTEM RESOURCES

How your operating system and applications use your computer's resources is another interesting point. While GNU/Linux and Windows both require a pretty hefty amount of disk space to install, GNU/Linux is much more flexible, and makes better use of your PC's resources. Some GNU/Linux distributions are small enough to fit on a floppy disk. Distributions like this are usually specialized for a particular purpose.

System Requirements for Windows XP *(per Microsoft's Web Site)*

- PC with 300 MHz or higher processor clock speed recommended; 233 MHz minimum required (single or dual processor system);* Intel Pentium/Celeron family, or AMD K6/Athlon/Duron family, or compatible processor recommended

- 128mb of RAM or higher recommended (64MB minimum supported; may limit performance and some features)

- 1.5 GB of available hard disk space*

- Super VGA (800 × 600) or higher-resolution video adapter and monitor

- CD-ROM or DVD drive

- Keyboard and Microsoft Mouse or compatible pointing device

If your system meets the requirements for Windows (listed above), chances are you'll be fine with GNU/Linux. The requirements for GNU/Linux actually vary, depending on your needs/wants. In fact, one can

---

still run GNU/Linux on older hardware, using 4-8 MB of RAM and 60-600 MB of hard disk space. Mind you, it won't be quite as exciting, but you **do** have more options.

Some GNU/Linux distributions actually fit onto the small business card CD's. Others can be booted from USB drives (assuming your BIOS allows that). Such distributions typically enable users to rescue crashed systems (even crashed Windows systems), experiment with GNU/Linux, or provide a limited set of applications that can be used when they don't otherwise have access to a complete GNU/Linux distribution. They're also great for demonstration purposes.

Of course, for churches, the ability to run GNU/Linux on older hardware could be very important. The hardware often donated to churches is sometimes as useful for a doorstop as anything else. With GNU/Linux, Emacs (a powerful text editor), and bc (a console-based spreadsheet) even the worst situations might be improved. Again, you might rather have a Graphical User Interface (GUI), but GNU/Linux is better than DOS when it comes to the command line!

GNU/Linux actually uses free RAM as a hard disk cache, to help reduce the number of times it has to go to your hard disk for data. Because going to the hard disk is relatively slow, this speeds things up a bit. It offers an efficient journaling filesystem, ReiserFS which would be the Windows equivalent of NTFS (NT Filesystem). ReiserFS can handle upwards of 17TB (Terabytes) of data – not that your church will ever use that much space.

GNU/Linux Applications generally require less disk space, less RAM, and create smaller files than their Windows counterparts. The MS Word version of this document is a full 100k larger than the OOo version. The Free Software Consortium's web site offers a document that points out significant differences between MS Office and OpenOffice.org. It is but one example of solid software development in the open source world.

The filesystem is likely the single most confusing aspect of GNU/Linux and UNIX in general. Here we'll introduce the basic GNU/Linux filesystem in a way that will help readers navigate it with ease. This discussion applies to the typical GNU/Linux system. While it may not be completely applicable across all UNIX or even all GNU systems, users will find below a fairly typical layout.

Let's talk first about disks and partitions. Windows uses letters to denote drives. Even partitions on a single hard drive are assigned drive letters. Since there are only 26 letters in the alphabet, it is possible (though highly unlikely) to run out of drive letters. There may well be ways of working around this, but Windows has never overcome this limitation.

Here are the typical Drive letter associations for Windows systems:

- A = 1st Floppy drive
- B = 2nd Floppy drive
- C = 1st Hard drive (every letter after this depends on the number of hard drives and partitions are part of the system.
- D = 1st CD-ROM drive (or 2nd Hard drive)

The CD-ROM/DVD-ROM (or any writable devices) drive is always the next letter after the last hard drive partition. Any additional drives take on the next available drive letter. Given a single hard drive in the computer with four partitions, the CD/DVD would be drive "G".

The root directory of the first partition on the hard drive would be denoted as "C:\". Windows is always installed on the "C" drive. Beneath that, most Windows systems have a few other folders:

- C:\Documents and Settings\username\My Documents
- C:\Program Files
- C:\Windows

The additional partitions can have whatever folders you create.

GNU/Linux considers most hardware to be devices of various sorts. Because GNU/Linux treats these devices as files, information about them is stored in the /dev directory. The first hard disk is referred to as "hda", and the second hard disk is referred to as "hdb". The first partition on the first hard drive is "hda1". Thus, /dev/hdb1 is the first partition of the second hard drive. Now keep all this in mind for a bit while we examine the filesystem proper.

The GNU/Linux filesystem takes a more flexible and informative approach than the Windows system. Whether a particular directory resides on the first partition of the first hard disk, or the sixth partition of the second hard disk may not be apparent to the end-user. This flexibility is transparent to the end-users. To them, it all looks like one single filesystem.

Typically, the GNU/Linux filesystem is broken up into various directories, all of which serve a purpose. Before you get too concerned about where to put your documents, users can't generally store their files outside of their "home" directories unless you give them permission to store them elsewhere. Let's look at the filesystem a little closer.

/

This is the root directory (not to be confused with root's directory, which we'll see below). It is the considered the main directory.

/bin

The "binaries" directory contains essential user commands.

/boot

The "boot" directory contains the information needed to start GNU/Linux when you turn on your computer.

/dev

The "device" directory contains all device files. As stated above, all devices are treated as files.

/etc

This directory contains the configuration files for most of the system, as well as a number of servers.

/home

The "home" directory contains the files for all users who have accounts (generally /home/jqpublic or similar).

/lib

The "libraries" directory contains programming libraries used by your applications.

/lost+found

In the unlikely event of a system crash, you may find lost data here.

/media

The "media" directory is where removable media, such as CDs, floppy disks, and USB drives are mounted.

/mnt

The "mount" directory is used mount external filesystems, such as those on another computer on the local network.

/opt

The "optional" directory frequently contains programs that are experimental or proprietary (or simply commercial). In the old days, this was used to install programs not installed with the operating system.

/proc

The "process" directory is really a virtual Filesystem, and does not take up hard drive space. Most system monitoring software gets information from here.

/root

This is the home directory of the system administrator (a.k.a. "Root" or root user).

/sbin

The "system binaries" directory contains binary files used by the system, and programs used only by the system administrator (root user).

/srv

The "services" (or server) directory is a fairly new directory that contains services, such as the Apache web server. For you web developers, it may also contain CGI-scripts. Be aware that different organizations may employ different schemes for this hierarchy.

/tmp

The "temporary" directory contains temporary files.

/usr

The "user" directory contains user programs and also the documentation (/usr/doc or /usr/share/doc)

/var

The "various" directory keeps logging and spooling data, among other bits of useful information.

While each directory is designed to store certain information, administrators have tremendous flexibility to use their own judgment. For example, some distributions install OpenOffice.org into /usr/local or in /opt. Others may install it into /usr/lib instead. All of these locations are valid and a matter of preference. Incidentally, this is part of why it is so difficult for viruses to do much damage to GNU/Linux systems. User documents should be stored within the realm of /home.

Software Maintenance & Upgrades

When developing software, programmers usually create files with code that can be re-used in other programs, called *libraries*. Programmers have a couple of options when it comes to taking advantage of a computer's resources. When developing for the Windows platform, most programmers typically include these libraries with their program. When developing for the GNU/Linux and UNIX platforms, programmers try to take advantage of libraries already available on the system. Let's consider the advantages and disadvantages of each.

When a Windows user installs a program, the installer usually offers a few options and then installs the files in the program's own directory. Users are oblivious of what is happening in the background. However, there are a couple of caveats to this approach. On the one hand, multiple copies of a library can be installed on the system. On the other hand, a program could copy a modified library over an existing copy of the same library.

Suppose a bug or security vulnerability is discovered in a library. If you update a single program that uses the library, you could still have other copies that have not been updated. Most users probably wouldn't even think to check whether other programs use the same library. If the other program vendors haven't offered updates of their own, the user may still be vulnerable.

When a library is overwritten by a new or modified version, you may not notice any difference until a much later period. Normally, an installer will notify users about conflicts, and offer the opportunity to keep the old file or overwrite it. It's probably safe to say that most users probably just choose to overwrite it, as the new program depends on the newer version. Just imagine the look on the Treasurer's face when the quarterly financial reports have not been updated because a library was updated during the installation of new software.

At the other end of the spectrum is the UNIX approach. Developers only include additional libraries when they need to write a new library for some function that the current selection doesn't offer. Otherwise, programs generally rely on the standard libraries already installed in the system. This approach reduces or eliminates the number of duplicate copies of libraries, and enables users to update the library once without impacting functionality of previously installed software.

This can, at times, present something of a challenge. Occasionally, a user may try to update a program, only to discover that it depends on a certain library, which in turn depends on another library. The result is what some have dubbed "dependency Hell". This is becoming less of a problem, as most package management software is able to help resolve the dependencies.

The Debian-based distributions, which use "Apt", have a solid reputation for practically eliminating the unfavorable problem of dependencies. Apt is so popular that there is now a version known as Apt for RPM, which works with the RPM-based distributions, like Red Hat, Fedora Core, SUSE, and Mandrake. The Yellow Dog Updater, Modified (a.k.a, YUM) is used by many Fedora Core users.

Computer Security

Securing your computers is a necessary task in today's rather hostile computing environment. Whether restricting access to sensitive information from staff and volunteers or preventing external attacks and viruses from bringing down your ministry's network, computer administrators need to be aware of the design issues and the capabilities of GNU/Linux, especially as compared to proprietary software. Bear in mind that GNU/Linux, unlike its proprietary counterparts, was designed from the ground up to be a multi-user, network operating system.

From a license perspective, open source software allows everyone access to the source code. Because so many eyes are examining the code, bugs and vulnerabilities are generally spotted and fixed much more rapidly than is possible with proprietary software. Proprietary software is open only to the vendors and the illegal hackers, who don't care much about license agreements anyway. This means only the vendor and the hackers know about vulnerabilities.

The question becomes, will the vendor step up and admit to the vulnerabilities and fix them? Or will the vendor hide them? With free and open source software you can get a patch, whether it comes from the vendor or elsewhere. If you have a developer in your ministry, you could even fix it yourself. You need to be careful that you get the patch from a reliable source, and in most cases you will want your patch to come from the developer.

From a design perspective, GNU/Linux has several advantages. GNU/Linux does not rely unnecessarily on remote procedure calls as some operating systems do. While some vendors have integrated their flawed web browsers into their operating systems, GNU/Linux will do no such thing – even with a reasonably secure web browser. Web browsers have nothing whatsoever to do with the operating system, and have no need to be "integrated" into it. Yet millions of computer users around the world continue to rely on an operating system with inherent design flaws.

Graphical user interfaces (GUIs, a.k.a. your desktop) have little or nothing to do with basic system tasks, yet some operating systems have an integrated GUI. Thus, when a graphical application hangs it affects the whole system. GNU/Linux keeps the GUIs separated from the underlying operating system. When a crash occurs, it rarely brings down the whole operating system. In most cases, the application or the desktop can be shut down without the need to reboot the whole computer.

The numerous viruses that exist generally attack one operating system. While some proclaim the popularity of the operating system fuels malicious attacks, the truth is that most attacks are aimed at proprietary systems with vulnerabilities, even though they represent less than half of the servers on the Internet. Frankly the bully concept comes to mind. Most bullies attack weak people because they are weak and vulnerable – not because they are popular. In other words, malware writers attack legacy operating systems because they can.

One would hope that the typical church or human services ministry would not need to worry about being exploited by local users. However, administrators cannot rule out the possibility of that happening. Not only do policies need to be established and implemented to help control access to sensitive information, administrators should be aware of a few issues pertaining to local system access.

By default, Microsoft Windows allows normal users write access to the whole filesystem, including the system directories. Whenever users click on the system folder in Windows Explorer, a message is displayed warning that important files are stored herein, and giving you the option to continue. This means that anyone can drop a malicious file into the system directory, although it is generally not even necessary, so long as the user that runs the malicious code has access. While the permissions can be changed, the default is usually accepted by administrators.

GNU/Linux allows read access to system directories, but not write access. The only person who has write access is root (unless permission is granted by root). So, for example, a normal user cannot generally rewrite the system configuration files stored in /etc. This does not mean that administrators can relax. However, their job is made that much easier by the default security settings of most GNU/Linux distributions.

Administrators will also want to control access to inappropriate content on the Internet. DansGuardian, Privoxy, and Squid (included with SUSE Linux) offer excellent firewall, privacy and content filtering services, and Privoxy runs on multiple operating system platforms. DansGuardian offers commercial support as well, for those who need it.

Administrators will want to learn about the GNU/Linux security tools, and monitor their system logs consistently. Even so, the design of GNU/Linux, along with the default settings of most distributions, offer better security and stability than some proprietary systems do. When you combine an operating system that makes it difficult for users to exploit with good security tools, you have a secure system. Maintaining a secure system is a major element in ensuring system and data integrity in any organization.

Now you have a little better understanding of how GNU/Linux uses your hardware, how the Filesystem is laid out, and how its design makes it more stable and secure. You know you can use the "mini distros", as they're often called, to rescue your system or access limited functionality. You also have a basic understanding of the more popular approaches to maintaining and upgrading your software. So what do you do when you need help? That's what the next chapter is all about.

10. SUPPORT OPTIONS

Perhaps one of the biggest stumbling blocks some churches will face is the perceived lack of quality technical support available for the GNU/Linux system and other free and open source software. People need to know how to get help, and the best resources on how to go about obtaining help might strike some Christians as a bit obtuse. Ministry staffers need to know how to get help, and we'll present that here in a useful way.

"Quality" is probably a better term than "professional" when talking about technical support. The term "professional" might refer to support by a polite, but under-trained (or inexperienced) help desk technician, which results in poor quality technical support. On the other hand, an experienced technician may not always be polite. It is important to recognize the difference between these two sides of the coin.

That the volunteer community often provides high quality support is really not so surprising given that many of the users who volunteer their time are actually computer professionals. By the same token, even fairly new users can be of some assistance to others. Most people won't answer if they aren't pretty sure their solution will work – their reputation is at stake.

That said, let's take a look at the various support options available to users of FOSS. Aside from the vast on-line documentation, users will find additional help from a supportive user community made up of professionals and enthusiasts alike. The community support options consist mostly of e-mail lists and web forums. Additionally, for those willing to pay for it, commercial technical support by telephone and e-mail is often available.

We will discuss each option in detail. However, users should know that there is a process by which we get help. If you purchase a technical support license from a commercial software distribution, feel free to get your money's worth by giving them a call. For those willing to rely on community support, you should, as a first step, consult your on-line documentation. If you cannot find a solution to your problem, or are confused by the information you find, you can ask the community with a reasonable degree of assurance that your question will be answered in a technically useful way.

The on-line documentation comes in a variety of forms. User can get help with commands by using the commands "*man*" or "*info*". These two commands are not generally considered to be very easy for most end-users, as they simply provide the command and its syntax. The How-To documents, normally found in a directory called /usr/share/docs, often provide much more detailed help for those who need it. These are generally easy to use and understand, and come in the form of a web page or in Adobe's PDF format.

There are a number of list-servs (e-mail lists)and web forums that offer users help with problems. The turn-around time on issues can be anywhere from 30 minutes to a couple of days, depending on the issue, the information provided about it and the time it takes someone with knowledge to respond. Each forum and list-serv has its own rules for posting questions. It is extremely important – if you want to solve your problem – to follow the guidelines for posting questions.

You should also be aware that there may be a number of ways to solve a single problem. For instance, I once posed a general question about setting up e-mail service for Oakdale's LAN, only to discover at least four different approaches, each with additional options. In a case like this, you can pick one option and stick with it until you get it working.

It is a good idea not to discuss your Christian faith in most forums and list-servs, as merely mentioning the word "church" can create quite a stir. What's more, technical forums are not the place to discuss religion, which can be freely discussed by those who care in appropriate forums. It is one thing to say that you are working on a computer for your church. It is quite another to start evangelizing in a technical forum.

The Christian FOSS community sites are the best places to mix theology and technology. Even here, you have to realize that most folks come from a wider range of theological backgrounds, and we have to respect each others' differences. Generally speaking, though, Christians will find a much warmer atmosphere in the Christian FOSS community. You can learn more about this community in the chapter devoted to it.

Using the On-Line Documentation (In-Depth)

There are a few different types of documentation available for GNU/Linux and BSD systems. The manual pages are great when you need help with command line utilities and some applications include their own help utility. Knowing which one to use in a given situation could help you find answers without having to rely on others.

The How-Tos tend to be tutorials. The How-Tos vary widely, and may take the form of web pages you can view in your web browser or Adobe's PDF format. A how-to may be a full-blown user manual or a step-by-step on how to install and configure a file server. The How-Tos are usually located in the directory (folder) /*usr/share/doc.*

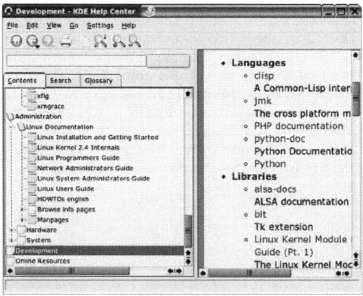

Illustration 9 - The KDE Help Center (SUSE 9.2)

The KDE and GNOME desktops generally have their own help systems, similar to the Windows help system. Commercial – and even non-profit – distributions may also customize those help systems to include helpful features. For instance, SUSE's KDE help system includes a way to browse the man and info pages from within your graphical shell. Illustration 9 (previous page) shows the KDE Help Center as it appears in SUSE Linux 9.2.

These desktop help systems generally offer user guides for the desktop and for applications that are specifically designed to run on that desktop. Getting help with KDE applications is a matter of using the help menu, and often brings up the KDE help system. Other applications use a help menu on their menu bar, and tend to offer their own, built-in utility for displaying the help information.

Every program can be run from a command line. On a Windows computer, with Microsoft WordPad (or any program), you can switch to the appropriate directory where WordPad is located, and type in the correct command to launch it. So try something similar to this:

```
C:\Program Files\WindowsNT\Accessories\wordpad
```

You can add options, such as a document name to the command, and have WordPad open a document at launch time. All commands, regardless of the operating system, have options and switches you can use to change the default behavior of the command. The way the command runs by itself is its *default* behavior. Consider an example using the *ps* command from GNU/Linux.

The *ps* command gives us a list of processes (processes are usually programs) currently running. The default behavior is to provide a list of processes running in the current shell. However, what if we would like to change its behavior a bit? In that case, we would use the *–h* or *--help* flags to find out what options are available to us.

The manual pages (or *man* pages), and *info* pages, offer a summary of a command and the options and switches available to it. To use these, simply type:

```
man command
man ps
```

The *info* command is used the same way.

Google is Your Friend

Google is an oft-used tool for searching e-mail list archives for answers to questions and challenges users face.

Using Google in the following way should yield some fairly useful results:

```
site:www.somesite.com keyword1 keyword2
site:lists.suse.com asus
```

This search finds information about the ASUS motherboards on the SUSE Linux e-mail archives site.

Use the "define:" keyword to find definitions for acronyms and other terms.

```
Define: term
define: ssh
```

This search brings up definitions of "ssh", which is the "secure shell", a secure alternative to Telnet. PuTTY is a Windows-based SSH client. Telnet and SSH allow users to login to a remote system and execute commands as if they were on that system.

There are a number of useful ways to use Google to solve problems. This applies to all software challenges as well. Regardless of whether your operating system doesn't recognize your printer or you can't figure out how to create filters in your e-mail client, you can always check Google as a starting point.

E-Mail Lists & Web Forums

Users have three options when it comes to asking questions: telephone support from their distribution vendor, e-mail lists and web forums. In most cases telephone technical support is included by commercial distributions to cover installation of the GNU/Linux operating system. Beyond that, you're best bet is typically to turn to e-mail lists (or list-servs) and web forums. Knowing how to ask the questions is every bit as important as knowing where to ask them.

The response time is not the same as if you pick up the phone, but it is a great deal cheaper, and frequently the help is at least as good, if not better than the phone support. Sometimes it is even faster. Typically, though, you should expect a 24-hour turn-around time on questions posted. However, the initial response may not solve your problem right away. You may need to work through a process to find your solution.

Before posting to an e-mail list, refer to the on-line documentation. There are two important reasons for this. The first is that you may find the answer to your problem. The second is that, if you don't, you'll be better prepared to ask your question than if you had just blurted out, "I can't start OpenOffice.org" in a user list. The first response (assuming you get one), will be to ask how you attempted to start OpenOffice.org, whether you're sure it is correctly installed, and so on.

It is difficult to help people who do not even understand their own problems. Once you've checked the documentation for your program, and attempted to find something on Google, the next step is to state the problem in terms that will let people know you have some idea about the problem. This will encourage those interested in helping you.

Below is an actual thread from the OpenOffice.org e-mail list. The original poster (OP) wants to know how to create two numbered lists, both starting with #1. He does not state what, if anything he has done to research the problem, but has nevertheless received a helpful response. For those not familiar with e-mail and newsgroup quoting, the ">>" refers to the original post. The ">" refers to the response. It apparently worked, or the thread would have continued until the issue was resolved.

>> I'm using 1.9.71.1

>>

> > How do I get Writer to restart numbering with 1 when

> > after a line (or more) with a style that is not the

> > numbering style?

>

> Format > Paragraph

> Numbering (tab)

> Restart at this paragraph (checkbox)

Thanks!

Because time is frequently a factor in getting help, you may be interested to know that the response to the "OP" took 25 minutes – about how long you might expect to sit on hold while waiting for a support technician, using paid technical support options. The original poster responded an hour later with the "Thanks" message. It can take a full day or more at times, but frequently does not. It all depends on the nature of the problem.

Such a post suggests to the audience, that you have researched your problem and are simply confused about something. From here, readers can begin to help you out. This link contains a helpful, if somewhat sarcastic discussion about asking questions in newsgroups and e-mail lists. It would also apply to web forums. http://www.catb.org/~esr/faqs/smart-questions.html

It is useful to know that almost every project available has either an e-mail list or a web forum available for its users. Many offer both services. Typically, there is an e-mail list for developers, and a separate list for users. List names may look something like: *myproject-users@myproject.org*

Linux Users Groups

At the local level, you may be able to find or start a Linux Users Group. Many larger cities have at least one, and others exist in local rural areas. Linux Users Groups often involve IT professionals, and some of these folks are Christians, or willing to help out a fellow GNU/Linux user. They usually hold a monthly meeting, where specific subjects are discussed. They may hold other events, such as "install-fests" where they help people install a GNU/Linux operating system.

These groups frequently have a website and an e-mail list where you can ask questions. You may also find computer hardware & software items to trade. How each group works depends largely on its charter, but it's a great way to network with local GNU/Linux users. While many of the folks involved in Linux Users Groups are not Christians, you're sure to find one or two in the crowd. Even if there are no Christians, you will usually find folks are willing to help you solve problems. After all, LUGs are a support network of sorts.

The Christian FOSS Community

The Freely Project offers an on-line help desk for churches and other ministries, and some members of The Freely Project are working to establish local support networks by working with local Linux Users Groups. The Freely Project is an advocacy website that offers technical support for free. It is a great resource for learning about various FOSS distributions. While we discuss the Christian FOSS community further in Chapter 14, it is worth noting here the Christian groups that offer technical assistance.

The help desk offers a ticket-based approach to helping users solve problems. Given the number of other resources available for individual users, the Freely Help Desk is only available to organizations. Users can submit a trouble ticket, and get an e-mail response with instructions. There is also a growing number of F.A.Q.s (Frequently Asked Questions) available to the users.

The Freely Project is working to establish local support networks through local members and/or Linux Users Groups where possible. While The Freely Project is still fairly small in numbers, there are members in various states in the U.S. and several other countries. If there is no member local to your area, you might find help through a local Linux Users Group.

Two e-mail lists serve Christians specifically. The ChristianSource – Free Software and Linux Users Group (CS-FSLUG) and Linux 4 Christians lists are excellent resources and include members from all over the world. Users include the very experienced and the very inexperienced. A number of women are involved in the lists – and not all of them are in the Information Technology field. A fair number of pastors also participate.

The essence of this chapter is that you should first check out the on-line documentation and search the web for information about your problem prior to asking for help. If you paid for technical support, it may still be worth looking into the documentation, but feel free to get your money's worth. If you post a question, be sure to offer some background, like you're hardware and software configuration, as well as the problem itself. Now that you know how to get help, let's find some software that Christians and churches can use.

11. FREE AND OPEN SOURCE SOFTWARE FOR THE CHURCH

Contrary to popular belief, which, to some extent, was supported by the previous edition of this book, there is quite a collection of free and open source software for Christians and churches. Bible study, church and worship management, and educational programs – not to mention standard office and Internet tools are available to Christians for use at home or in the church. Let's examine some of the applications available to users, including a few that run on proprietary operating systems.

It is important to note that many of the available applications support multiple operating systems, and frequently multiple spoken languages as well. Applications range from the simple to the complex, both in terms of purpose and use. Furthermore, some of the tools available to Christians are cutting edge technology, designed to serve specific missions-oriented needs. The applications we address here may not be the only ones, but certainly are some of the most important free and open source applications available to Christians.

Bible Study Applications

The CrossWire Bible Society sponsors The Sword Project, which offers Bible study applications for several operating systems. The Sword project provides Bible translations, commentaries and other reference texts as modules. Several sub-projects develop platform-specific (and platform independent) applications to access the modules, thus providing Bible study tools for a wide range of operating systems.

The Sword for Windows project is available for Windows users. MacSword obviously is the Bible study tool for the Mac operating system. BibleTime and GNOMESword are GNU/Linux versions of the Sword Project. JSword/Bible Desktop is a Java-based Bible study tool that runs on any platform with Java installed. You will discover that each project supports a wide range of features, but not necessarily all of the features. BibleTime supports the personal commentary, and those that have not yet built in support for that will be doing so in the near future.

Crosswire also hosts forums and e-mail lists for the Sword projects and Ichthux, a new Debian-based GNU/Linux project aimed at Christians and churches. Users without a broadband Internet connection may want to order a CD that contains all of the Sword software. It sure beats waiting for that multi-megabyte encyclopedia module to download.

One can use the Settings menu in BibleTime (Illus. 10) to launch the Sword configuration utility. From there, the click of a button will connect you to the Sword Project website, where you can choose a Bible, commentary, or other module to install. To use the personal commentary, simply right-click on it in the module pane, and select whether to edit it using plain text or HTML. You don't have to know HTML; BibleTime just displays it as such.

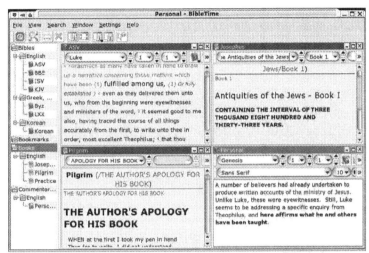

Illustration 10 - BibleTime with ASV, Josephus, Pilgrim's Progress, and the personal commentary

The Flashcards project is useful for advanced Bible students, laypeople and clergy alike. Use it to memorize Biblical Greek words. A number of the folks on the e-mail lists use and love Flashcards. Because it is Java-based, it will run on any computer with Java installed. This is highly advantageous when you run one operating system at the church and another at home.

Thus, regardless of what operating system you use, you'll always have a decent open source Bible study application available to you. Some publishers have not made their works available, and thus such tools are inaccessible to the Christian FOSS community. More will be said about this in Chapter 14.

Church Management Applications

Let's get down to one issue that really matters to churches – the church management software. There are two general options for free and open source church management software. InfoCentral and its variants, Open Source Church and ChurchInfo, are currently web-based applications. CHADDB is a simple database back-end for MySQL. Users can currently use OpenOffice.org to connect to CHADDB via the JDBC driver, and a Java-based front-end is currently in development.

InfoCentral's lead developer is developing the next version using Java/J2EE for larger churches. Being in the early stages, no release date is set. Even so, the new application will include a full set of financial tools for churches. That functionality will be an important factor for most large churches. The InfoCentral team may also provide professional technical support.

None of the Windows-based companies are moving to port their applications to GNU/Linux. The GNU/Linux community might jump in and help to meet this need. Some, such as Info Central (and my own CHADDB), are trying to meet the needs using MySQL and PHP, but others will need to pitch in and help out. Churches should encourage their vendors to consider porting their applications to GNU/Linux.

InfoCentral/ChurchInfo/Open Source Church

InfoCentral is a web-based church management project that uses the PHP scripting language, and can be used in any web browser, making it very appealing for end-users. Web-based solutions like this involve setting up a web server, a database server, and then running the scripts to configure the application. It may take a little work to setup, but is easy for users to use in day-to-day operations.

InfoCentral's lead developer decided to take InfoCentral to the Java platform, keeping it portable and improving scalability. This decision has led to a couple of spin-offs from the InfoCentral project, such as ChurchInfo and Open Source Church. InfoCentral, in its current PHP form has been used by a church with 2000 members, and is currently in use by hundreds of churches around the world.

ChurchInfo (www.churchdb.org) appears to be most like the InfoCentral application, and has added new functionality. Attendance can be tracked using a barcode. Donations can be automated by bank draft and credit card. Pledges and donations can be tracked by family. The image below shows part of the form used to add a family in ChurchInfo.

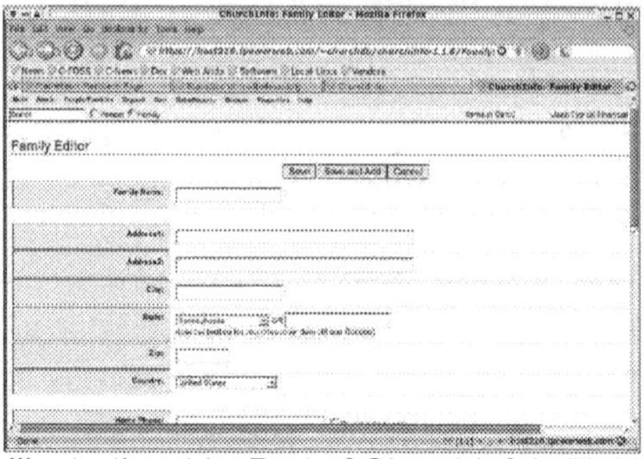

Illustration 11 - Part of ChurchInfo's "Add a Family" form

Open Source Church also remains similar to InfoCentral, and offers a service hosting church databases on their web site. While it is possible to keep data fairly secure, many churches are hesitant to keep their data where it is more vulnerable to attack. Still, churches can use web-based solutions like this right in their own offices. Web-based solutions keep the data in a central location and are easily accessed over the church network.

CHADDB – The CHurch ADministration DataBase

CHADDB (pronounced like chaddy-bee) is simply a database back-end designed for the MySQL database server. As such, any kind of front-end can be used for it. Currently, a Java-based front-end is being developed and CHADDB can be used "as is" with OpenOffice.org. CHADDB provides basic church management functions, and will be developed to add further functionality.

Connecting OpenOffice.org to CHADDB is simply a matter of using the JDBC driver to establish the connection to the MySQL database. It requires a few steps, but is accomplished easily enough once all the components are in place. Data can be extracted from CHADDB directly into any document you create in OpenOffice.org.

Illustration 12 - Creating a form letter in OpenOffice.org using CHADDB as the data source

Above is a sample form letter created simply by dragging and dropping the column headings from the data source viewer (shown above the document) into the document at the insertion point. When this letter is printed, each copy will have the proper name and address where you see the fields. The data source viewer shows a simple address book query that has been created using two tables from CHADDB.

Church management programs are few and far between. However, the available solutions are flexible and free (as in free coffee and freedom). ChurchInfo and Open Source Church are the most mature projects. CHADDB provides basic functionality to work with OpenOffice.org. Developers are encouraged to pitch in with the current projects, as well as to build a native GNU/Linux front-end for CHADDB.

As of OpenOffice.org 2.0, churches may opt for the Access-like OOBase. While Base is definitely new, it offers churches an easy way to build and use their own databases. None of the available tools provides a complete system. However, all of the tools offer serious functionality or the ability to develop your own. As much as some people gripe about their church management software, that should be worth something.

Worship Software

Asaph & PyAsaph

Asaph is a Java-based song database, and is thus multi-platform. The developer is a Seattle, Washington worship leader who wrote Asaph to meet his own need. Asaph enables users to print songbooks, sheets or transparencies with or without chord markings. PyAsaph, developed by South African believer, David Fraser, adds lyric projection capabilities.

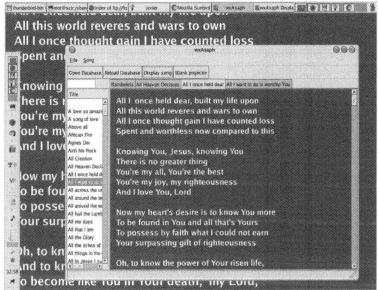

Illustration 13 - PyAsaph shown on a Fedora Core system with the admin screen and the actual display in the background

Lyricue

Lyricue is a lyrics projection application for GNU/Linux systems. Compared to its proprietary counterparts Lyricue only lacks moving backgrounds and integration with PowerPoint. Moving backgrounds could be added soon. Integration with OpenOffice.org Impress would be an excellent improvement. One church sound technician uses Lyricue to handle his church's lyrics projection and Audacity to record services, which are later burned to CD.

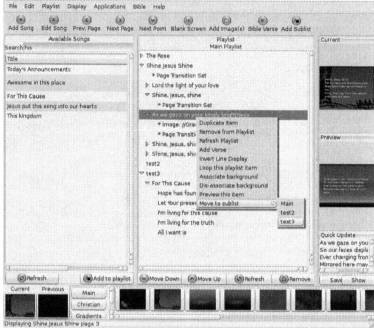

Illustration 14 - Lyricue's main screen

OpenLP

OpenLP is a Windows-only application used by a large number of churches.. OpenLP users can download songs using Christian Copyright Licensing International's SongSelect feature. It supports several languages, making it useful in a number of countries and in churches with multi-lingual ministries. The image below shows the main screen. The left side shows the preview and live modes, so the technician can view the results of changes before sending them out to the live feed. Users can quickly select songs using the database in the middle.

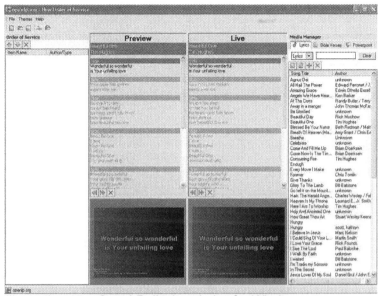

Illustration 15 - OpenLP displays lyrics for Windows users.

Illustration 16 - The OpenLP display screen, shown using a "dual-head" (dual monitor) setup.

The Above image shows the display screen. While OpenLP is Windows-only at the moment, a port to GNU/Linux is planned. Developers who are interested in helping with the port project should contact the lead developer.

OpenSong

OpenSong runs on Mac and Windows systems, but also on GNU/Linux with a little work. A thread (discussion) on the subject appears on the project's SourceForge site. It's not quite as well supported as the Windows version. Version 1.0 is due out soon with better GNU/Linux support promised. OpenSong is apparently very popular with its users.

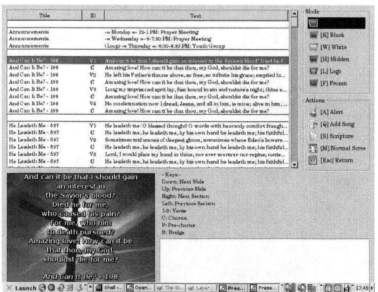

Illustration 17 - OpenSong's display control window (running on Xandros Desktop)

GNU/Linux Distros

Apologetix

Apologetix is the brainchild of, Preston Boyington, a Mississippi (USA) believer who had involved the youth of his church's ministry. He had also managed to garner support from various sources, only to see much of this support erode a short time later. The project continues to progress slowly, and could – potentially, at least – unite with the Ichthux project.

Ichthux

Ichthux is what is known in the Debian community as a Custom Debian Distribution. That is, it is Debian, albeit customized for a specific purpose or market segment. The first edition of this book inspired at least two Christians to begin developing a customized GNU/Linux distribution for churches. One of these, and others with similar goals, have since discovered each other and combined efforts.

Ichthux is the result. Biblix and Ixthus, along with a Damn Small Linux-based project (DSL is a min-distro that fits on a business card CD) were all Debian-oriented efforts. The current version is not yet at 1.0, and thus may not be usable by a wide audience. Even so, believing geeks will surely enjoy playing with Ichthux.

http://ichthiux.free.fr/wikini/wakka.php?wiki=Main

Educational Applications

Commercial GNU/Linux systems typically include plenty of educational software that churches can put to good use in after school programs or in their own Bible schools. Programs for Math, Astronomy, and foreign language studies should be easy to use for those who understand the concepts of each field. Here, though, we'll mention two programs specifically. Gcompris is a fun learning tool with bright colors. Moodle is in use by universities and missions organizations alike.

The educational software should open doors for many families as well. Those that cannot afford commercial proprietary programs can count on GNU/Linux applications to help their children keep pace – or even excel – in today's educational rat race. Much of it could be used in home and private school environments as well.

GCompris

For kids aged 2-10 years old, GCompris is an excellent multi-discipline educational program that uses activity boards. Children can develop their mouse skills, learn the alphabet and arithmetic operations, and play educational games. Boards have a modular function in that you can pick and choose the boards you want to use. People can develop additional boards to be added to the collection.

http://gcompris.free.fr/

Moodle

Moodle (Modular Object-Oriented Dynamic Learning Environment) is a highly rated web-based distance learning application (generally referred to as Course (or Learning) Management Systems). A number of Christian organizations are deploying Moodle, which supports at least 50 languages. Moodle includes a number of add-on modules that enhance its functionality.

http://www.moodle.org/

General Applications

Audacity

Audacity is a sound recording program that runs on GNU/Linux, Mac, and Windows systems, and offers numerous features, including recording live audio, editing audio files in a variety of formats, and the ability to convert tapes or records to digital recordings.

www.audacity.org

Ardour

Ardour is a complete Digital Audio Workstation that allows users to record, edit and mix multi-track audio, produce CD's, video soundtracks and more. It is even capable of mastering projects to completion.

http://ardour.org/

Rosegarden

Rosegarden is a general purpose music composition and editing environment that includes score editing, along with audio and midi sequencing. Rosegarden will likely be ideal for most church musicians with an interest in composing general music.

www.rosegardenmusic.com

LilyPond

LilyPond is music typesetting software, enabling users to create "engraved" musical score sheets in the classical music tradition. LilyPond is a batch program that takes musical commands you enter in a text file, and produces a score sheet as the final result.

http://lilypond.org/web/index.html Asterisk

Asterisk

Asterisk is a PBX system for GNU/Linux. When used with Digium's Wildcard TDM400P card ($100-$340), churches and other organizations have the ability to run a full-featured PBX system with support for up to four lines. Asterisk works with other hardware and supports additional phone lines. It is now available for Microsoft Windows as well.

www.asterisk.org

12. MIGRATION
STRATEGIES

The decision to migrate to GNU/Linux involves examining each of the major challenges we have examined thus far. It also involves considering the best strategy to use for completing a migration. The best approach is probably a gradual one for most organizations, except those just getting started with computers. You need to consider which distribution and what application set you want to use. Ultimately, your strategy will depend on the size and technical abilities of your organization, as well as how much you have invested in proprietary software.

In this chapter, we'll provide a brief overview of the gradual approach most recommended by those with experience in software migration. We'll also examine the most important facets of the migration process, including user comfort. We will address new ministries and other organizations separately. We'll also discuss the use of outside consultants or other "experts", as there are some things you should understand about "IT experts".

Whatever you do, it might be a good idea to create a fairly small team. The team should consist of the most capable person in your church, where computers are concerned, at least one staff member, and at least one non-technical person who has an open mind and is willing to do a bit of research. I suggest the non-technical person because this person will help your migration team understand how the new software will impact them. Additionally, your team could include any outside consultants you choose to hire to assist you.

Incidentally, your team may need or want to work at a personal level – that is, without much support from the church – to study the issues involved initially. If, after all the homework has been done, the church chooses not to migrate to GNU/Linux, the migration team should be assigned to continue watching the free and open source software community for future opportunities. In other words, always keep the door open to a potential migration.

Reasons to migrate

In order to facilitate any movement in the direction of free and open source software we need to first understand why we are migrating. Although that has been the point of the previous chapters, let's simply summarize some of the main issues. After all, if we don't understand why we are migrating, then we are merely conducting an exercise in change management.

One important reason is to rid our ministries of the proprietary traps that imprison us in an expensive, restrictive license agreement. Proprietary software makes migrating to any other solution more difficult and expensive than it needs to be. Proprietary software keeps us stuck with a single vendor – a great thing until that vendor raises the prices on its software. Changing from that proprietary vendor to another is more difficult than migrating from one FOSS vendor to another.

The ability to choose between vendors gives you bargaining power. In fact, if the cost of migrating costs more than upgrading, that is only an initial investment. You are really investing in the ability to negotiate better prices in the future. You are also investing in an overall reduced cost of computing – and we should not lose sight of that goal. If the cost of the migration is less than the cost of upgrading, you essentially have capitalized on your savings. The freedom to change vendors when necessary is difficult to calculate in your budget, but the impact is phenomenal.

The typical proprietary license restricts our freedom unnecessarily. Many people violate these licenses in spite of the hefty penalties. Whenever Christians have the choice to use software in violation of a legally binding agreement, or to use free and open source software, we should choose the latter, which legally permits us to use the software in ways proprietary software does not. For Christians, free and open source software, by their nature, harmonize with Christian values and principles in a way that proprietary software cannot do.

Another excellent reason for migrating is security. We can reduce our vulnerability to viruses, reduce the impact of external attacks on our systems, and better protect our systems from internal attacks. Certain proprietary vendors continue to suffer from security vulnerabilities, due in no small part to their design methodology. The need to purchase additional software tools to protect legacy operating systems adds to the cost of maintaining them.

Extending the abilities of your current hardware resources can be one reason to migrate. Ease of use can be another. XFce, the lightweight graphical desktop, allows you to maximize your system performance while offering a minimum of desktop toys to confuse your users. Flexibility is demonstrated in the choice of graphical desktops, all of which can be customized to look and act an awful lot like Windows (or not). It is also demonstrated in the choice of productivity applications available.

Adherence to open standards is yet another reason. Got a Japanese document in OpenOffice.org format? Microsoft Office cannot open it. OpenOffice, StarOffice[4], KOffice, and others support and use the OpenDocument format – a format soon to be an ISO standard. Networking protocols, security protocols, and a number of other standards are in place. Proprietary software vendors typically adopt open standards, and then add their own proprietary innovations, thus making interoperability expensive and difficult, or even impossible.

Most Internet protocols, like HTTP, FTP, and others are open standards by which any computer can communicate with any other computer, regardless of the operating system or even client software involved. Unfortunately, some companies do not want to cooperate, making it nigh impossible to interoperate with their software. They do this intentionally. Sadly, many users reward them by using their software, rather than rejecting the closed standard.

---

4   StarOffice is a non-free version of OpenOffice.org.

We see a number of reasons to migrate, all of which have been elaborated further in previous chapters. Here we have simply summarized the reasons for migrating. Now let's consider the gradual approach to migration. The gradual approach is the most-recommended approach, and is best used in established ministries with a heavy investment in proprietary software. Newer and smaller ministries will be able to start out with GNU/Linux or migrate fairly quickly by comparison.

The Emotional Element

Perhaps the biggest obstacle to any migration is user comfort with the current software. Many users seem to assume that something new is simply over their heads, even if it isn't. The more adventurous users will be better able to handle change, while those less technically inclined will be more apprehensive about change. The initiative and motivation to change will need to come from the church leadership.

The fact that we already know a particular program – and are somewhat attached to it is neither the best nor the only factor in a change scenario. There certainly is something to be said for being proficient with the tools we use. However, proficiency often becomes a euphemism for our emotional comfort level. We will again become proficient with new tools. We may even wonder why we didn't start with the new tools much earlier.

Most of the changes that the user will notice are more cosmetic than technical. The technical differences do exist, and some common tasks are accomplished using a slightly different process. However, the real problem of change is the change itself – not the software. Church leaders simply need to be prepared to help deal with the change aspect. A great many migrations encounter very little resistance once underway.

Church leaders can help by encouraging the staff. Providing a little hand-holding assistance could prove quite beneficial, not only from a financial standpoint, but also from an emotional perspective. Whoever is leading the migration should keep a good sense of humor about them, and avoid belittling the folks wrestling with change.

The Gradual Approach

The gradual approach essentially involves first migrating to FOSS applications that run on your current, legacy operating system software. Just a few examples are OpenOffice.org, Firefox, Thunderbird, and MySQL. Don't forget the church-related applications mentioned in Chapter 11. Meanwhile your migration team can study GNU/Linux closely, and even play with different distributions using the popular live evaluation CDs. Once users are comfortable using the new applications, then replacing the underlying operating system is much easier.

Probably the best place to begin is with Firefox and Thunderbird. Remove the Internet Explorer Icon from the desktop, and get them using Firefox instead. You should make Internet Explorer available through the Start Menu, as some websites are designed for it exclusively. The lack of security vulnerabilities makes Firefox the ideal starting point for your migration. It shouldn't take long for them to get comfortable with it.

A little later you can install OpenOffice.org next to Microsoft Office. Be ready to point out the differences between Microsoft Office and OpenOffice.org. The OpenOffice.org website has documents that point out some of these differences (see the Resources at the end of this book for the link to OOo/MSO differences). Having the staff open the church bulletin and other frequently used documents in OpenOffice.org and make changes where appropriate would be an excellent way to help them get the feel of the new office suite.

Actually, installing OpenOffice.org can be accomplished at the same time as Firefox and Thunderbird. However, doing so could throw your users a bit more of a curve ball than they're ready for. You could give your more adventurous users both the new Internet tools and the new office suite at the same time. Some, though, will find too much new stuff a little overwhelming.

After your users have gotten used to the Windows-based free and open source applications you can begin to introduce the new operating system. They will need to get used to the virtual desktops, as well as "mounting" and "un-mounting" removable media. You will want to show them little tricks, like switching consoles and so forth.

The time line for a gradual migration could be up to a year, depending on your situation. I would suggest letting your users spend about a month or two with Firefox and Thunderbird before adding OpenOffice.org. In the second or third month, add OpenOffice.org, and give users another three to six months with it. Optionally, you could run OpenOffice.org next to Microsoft Office for a short period, and then remove the latter after a few months.

In about the eighth or ninth month, you can begin installing a pure GNU/Linux environment, albeit for one user at a time. Since GNU/Linux works across the network with Windows computers this is the best approach. Running a dual-boot configuration is probably best for the early study and preparation phase. However, if you need to run a Windows program under GNU/Linux, you will need to use the dual-boot configuration.

Choosing Your New Desktop Environment

You will want to begin exploring your GNU/Linux distribution options at the soonest possible time. Some distributions can be a little daunting for new users to install, but are very easy to keep up to date. Others are very easy to install, but a little challenging to keep up to date. You'll want to consider the bells and whistles included with each distribution, including the various levels of commercial technical support.

If you just want to try out all this *GNU* stuff, you should obtain Knoppix, Morphix, and/or Ubuntu. Ichthux should be a viable option in the near future. These are live, evaluation distributions that run off the CD, rather than from your hard drive. This gives users the chance to try GNU/Linux without actually installing it to their systems. You may be able to save documents you create in your Live CD trials to your floppy drive.

Incidentally, many people have used Knoppix to recover their crashed Windows systems. Additionally, SUSE offers a live CD. Be aware that the Free Software Foundation does not recommend these since they include non-free software. Most ministries will want to avoid using non-free software. The only GNU/Linux distributions known to include only free software are Ututo-e and Dynebolic. Other distributions may offer live CDs as well. You can also order CD sets that include a basic copy of several distributions.

While the *Guide to GNU/Linux Distributions* section in the back of this book will help you further, here are a few thoughts about choosing your distribution. Fedora Core, Linpsire, Mandrake, SUSE, and Xandros Desktop appear to be the best options for most new users. Debian and Slackware will be more suitable for the technically inclined and the skilled users. Morphix and Ubuntu offer the strengths of Debian along with the ease of installation of the other distributions.

You will almost certainly want to decide on a single workstation setup for all users. Aside from limiting how much software you need to install, a unified setup will simplify technical support issues. If you want to give users a choice in which desktop they'll use, you can involve them in the desktop trials, giving them a chance to play with different desktop environments, such as KDE, GNOME, and XFce. With your choice of distribution and desktop made you only need to select the various software packages to install.

Most distributions offer the option to setup a simple workstation during the installation process. In many cases, you will want to choose the detailed package selection mode to install individual packages that you know you want. You will need to do some research to determine which packages you want, as it would be difficult to describe the thousands of programs included in most distributions. Suffice it to say that you will likely want most of the software mentioned in this book.

GNU/Linux distributions tend to offer multiple programs for a single task. The goal is to offer you the choice. It is not necessary to install multiple office suites or database servers. Ordinarily, OpenOffice.org or KOffice will work. Since KOffice is almost always installed by default, you may want to de-select it, and ensure that OpenOffice.org is selected. The same rule applies to most other software included on the installation media. You don't have to install everything, but you can (in most cases) if you want to.

One case where you cannot install multiple programs is that of your printing system. Here you can use either, the old UNIX system (lp), or CUPS. CUPS should be the default option these days, and is what you will want to use. CUPS is a modern printing system that supports far more hardware than the old system. There may be situations where the old system offers advantages, but you will need to check up on that. CUPS is best for most people.

Hardware Upgrade Approach

Some ministries will find it makes more sense to migrate to GNU/Linux when they upgrade their hardware next. This is a very sensible approach, as ministries can specify GNU/Linux-compatible hardware, and prepare staff and volunteers in advance. It is also ideal, as the church can rely on a knowledgeable vendor to install the operating system, thus receiving a turn-key solution.

Whether or not all computers are upgraded simultaneously is of little importance. GNU/Linux can act as a server for Windows workstations, or connect to a Windows network using SAMBA, the open source implementation of Microsoft's file and print service protocol. We have discussed OpenOffice.org's ability to handle Microsoft Office documents previously. This is a good time to install OpenOffice.org on the Windows computers, as it provides an opportunity for the users still using Windows to begin getting comfortable with the new office suite.

This is either an all-at-once or a piecemeal approach, depending on how you upgrade your hardware. Either way, it affords an opportunity to prepare for the change. One advantage of deploying GNU/Linux with new hardware is that you can simply tell your hardware vendor to use only hardware known to work with GNU/Linux.

New and Small Ministries

New and small ministries may have the greatest opportunities for migrating to GNU/Linux. Many ministries are just starting with computers or have yet to purchase a proprietary church management database. GNU/Linux provides these churches to accomplish the same tasks that larger churches perform, albeit without the hefty financial investment in proprietary software. This is a church's best opportunity to start with, or to migrate to, a purely free and open source software platform.

The reason that going with GNU/Linux is ideal for new and smaller ministries is that most have very little invested in their computing platform. It is the ideal opportunity to get started and save serious money in the long term. As your ministry grows, you'll be able to focus on better hardware for the lyrics display and recording aspects of your worship ministry. Whatever ministry challenges you face, you can still have quality software while focusing on your ministry.

If you're about to buy new computers, simply head over to Wal-Mart and order their Linspire computers. These may be available only from the website (www.walmart.com), but you can check with your local store for more information. You can also check local custom computer shops, many of whom will be able to pre-install one distribution or another for you. It is a great opportunity to establish a relationship with a local business that may be able to provide a certain level of local support.

Perhaps the real challenge for smaller ministries is the typical lack of members with computer skills. Typically, whoever can do the word processing becomes the computer expert by default – even when they only know a little about word processing. Your only computer literate member may barely know Windows, and has probably never even heard of GNU/Linux. If you happen to be one of the few ministries that do have a GNU user in the midst, put them to work!

If you don't already have a GNU/Linux user in your church, you'll need to find someone willing to learn about it and play with it a bit. Help them to find the local Linux Users Group, and provide whatever additional information you can. Again, your volunteer does not need to be a technical genius to begin the adventure. They simply need to be willing to commit some time and effort to it.

Getting a Windows-only user, or any non-technical person up and running as your GNU/Linux administrator could take a little time. That's O.K. Churches rarely have the need to rush that most businesses might face. Again, look for Linux Users Groups and refer to the chapter on technical support options. The Christian free and open source software community is an excellent resource with plenty of patient folks willing to help others learn.

A new or small ministry with any technical expertise at all should be able to migrate or get going almost immediately. If a member can install Windows, it is highly likely they will be able to install GNU/Linux, especially one of the commercial distributions. The main task will be saving all documents to a CD (or a few CDs) so that you can open them in OpenOffice.org later.

Working with the Experts

It is not generally necessary to obtain the services of an expert. However, doing so could boost your comfort level significantly and may even reduce the cost of a migration. Using a consultant could help you to make a short-term migration, provide some basic training for your staff, and reduce the fear-factor involved with change. If the consultant cannot help you reduce the cost of a migration, you probably should seek to do it yourself. Even so, remember that you are investing in your computing future, meaning it may be worth the extra cost in the long run.

As mentioned in the beginning of this book, some people seem to think that getting an "expert" opinion from someone on their job is all the answer they need. However, most of the IT "experts" I know are Windows experts who know little or nothing about GNU/Linux. Guys with far more experience than I have in information technology are lost when I speak of NFS (the Network filesystem). They are highly intelligent people; they just don't have experience with GNU/Linux.

Look for someone who does have experience with GNU/Linux. While you certainly want the more mature folks in the crowd, don't discount that teen-ager who runs GNU/Linux at home. One of the volunteers with

The Freely Project Help Desk is a 16-year-old who is more knowledgeable about GNU/Linux than a number of the so-called "IT experts" who really are only Windows experts.

This is truly an important issue. While most Windows technicians will be able to better grasp the differences between GNU/Linux and Windows, many simply cannot tell you whether you should or should not migrate to GNU/Linux. Most of them don't even know what applications and utilities exist for GNU/Linux. Yet, many people rely on their advice to make a decision about whether or not to migrate to GNU/Linux.

At the very least, you need someone who has used both operating systems fairly extensively. Anyone who has not used GNU/Linux for at least a full year really cannot say much. You should look for folks who know the desktop workstation aspect, as well as the server aspect of GNU/Linux. Ironically, most GNU/Linux users do know Windows, as many started with it. Of course, many still run GNU/Linux and Windows in a dual-boot configuration, if only to keep abreast of Windows developments.

Preferably, your expert would be able to help you determine which e-mail client would provide the best solution. Evolution and Kontact are equivalents to Microsoft Outlook. On the other hand, there is Thunderbird, which will soon have a well-developed calendar function. Sylpheed-Claws is an excellent e-mail client that may be overlooked.

Your expert may not know all the software you need. For example, some folks may be able to help you install Audacity, even if they don't know anything about music reproduction. Your own music expert will likely be able to pick up on Audacity quickly, and may even know it already. Yet, the expert should be able to help you determine which programs will best suit your needs.

Finally, if you sign an agreement with a professional consultant, you should ensure that they show you how to perform maintenance tasks on your own. Backing up your system, checking your logs, and maintaining any network security in place are some critical tasks you will need to perform yourself. A good place to start is with the local Linux Users Group. Just don't rely on a Windows-only expert to be your guide.

13. GNU/LINUX
BACKGROUND

Richard Stallman started out with free software, even though that label had not yet been applied. He watched as the free software developer community collapsed, and determined that it would be necessary to create an entire operating system so that one could run a computer using nothing but free software. He began the GNU Project in 1984, quitting his position at MIT Labs to ensure that MIT could not claim ownership of the work. Stallman first wrote GNU Emacs (a text editor) and distributed it for $150.

After Emacs, the GNU Project began work on a free compiler, a tool programmers use to translate their source code into machine-readable, binary code. They developed a C library, a shell (Bash), GNU Tar (for archiving files), and other tools. By 1990, the GNU Project had most of the software needed to run a computer on nothing but free software. Now they needed a kernel.

The Hurd was to be GNU's kernel, but was not due to be released anytime soon. The idea is to deploy several servers on top of a micro-kernel. The Hurd attempts to fully implement the principles of sound operating system design. Although today, there are GNU distributions using the Hurd kernel, it is not as mature or stable yet as Linux. Meanwhile Stallman and others had developed most of the other software needed to make a complete operating system. With the Hurd still under development, GNU needed a kernel.

Linus Torvalds, a student at the University of Helsinki, in Finland, began work on Linux in 1991. He intended it to be a hobby operating system, never imagining that he would have such a dramatic impact on the world. He wanted a UNIX-like system that he could run on his 386 computer at the time. Minix was available gratis, but was restrictive and technically inadequate. He wrote Linux using the tools already available from Richard Stallman's GNU Project and released it under the GPL. Finally, in 1992, GNU was combined with Linux, to form the complete GNU/Linux system.

Version 1.0 was released in 1994, and the kernel (the heart of any operating system) has reached version 2.6 as of this writing. The even number of the kernel version is important as a stability indicator. Odd-numbered kernels (2.1, 2.3, etc.) are considered development releases, while the even-numbered kernels are the stable releases. This convention may or may not apply to other software. You should check with the developers to find out about their versioning schemes. Users are free to download whichever version they want, but the development versions are probably best left for the tech guys.

While GNU/Linux was initially a hobby system, it has gained popularity, not only among geeks, but also among business technology managers. Businesses and governments alike, especially in overseas markets, are migrating to GNU/Linux. Several GNU/Linux vendors offer business case pages on their web sites. A Christian denominational headquarters in Germany is using SUSE Linux Open Exchange Server to manage communication. Many American Small Office/Home Offices (SOHOs) are running GNU/Linux.

GNU/Linux is used almost exclusively by the movie industry, and has been used producing numerous movies, including *Lord of the Rings, Scooby Doo*, and *Star Wars Attack of the Clones*. Likewise, the NASA Space Center in Houston, Texas uses GNU/Linux in a variety of ways. Many non-profits use GNU/Linux and other free and open source software in their organizations. One group of churches is about to launch a website where they will make all of their in-house materials available under free and open terms.

School systems across America are migrating to GNU/Linux because of the ability to better control security, in addition to the cost factor. This includes private, as well as public schools. The Linux Terminal Server Project (LTSP) is being deployed widely. SUSE Linux has a SUSE In Schools program. Several articles have been written about using GNU/Linux in schools that have suffered legal trouble stemming from the improper use of proprietary software.

Johnson C. Smith University, in Charlotte, North Carolina, uses the Moodle educational portal that runs on multiple platforms. Christian missionary support organizations are deploying Moodle as a way to provide educational material to their missionaries. TechMission, a Christian organization that funds Christian Community Computing Centers around the United States, offers a free software CD to member organizations.

GNU/Linux is not just for organizations. Many of the people who use it are home users. Parents report that their children love the games. There are programs for just about every task you need to accomplish. One young guy I know watched T.V. on his SUSE Linux computer. CD and DVD burning software are included. Accessing the Internet is what GNU/Linux is made for. And whatever else you need that is not included in your distribution is almost surely available for download from the Internet.

Linux has a mascot – a penguin named Tux, who appears to have just had his fill of fish. Tux is intended to convey friendliness to new users. Tux is represented a bit differently by each distribution and Linux User Group (LUG). There are even depictions of Tux based on nationality. You may, of course, purchase all sorts of accessories, from t-shirts to ties that show off your Linux pride.

The GNU Project also has a mascot – the gnu (wildebeest). The gnu is not as widely recognized as the penguin, but certainly symbolizes a break from the herd mentality. The GNU Project sponsors many software projects, all in various stages of development, and sells software CDs. The Free Software Foundation is the GNU Project's sister organization that serves as the advocacy arm.

The Open Source Initiative is an organization similar to the Free Software Foundation, and approves open source licenses. It started as an effort to clarify misunderstandings about free software, thus coining the term "open source". However, as explained earlier in the book, that term is not completely synonymous with free software. Notwithstanding, the Open Source Initiative offers a strong business case for developing open source software.

It was the folks behind the Open Source Initiative who helped bring about the Mozilla and Firefox web browsers. While there are philosophical differences between the Free Software Foundation and the Open Source Initiative, they remain a strong alliance in the face of a largely proprietary software arena.

There is certainly more to the story than I could possibly tell here. You can explore the depths of GNU/Linux on your own. Hopefully this little bit of insight into GNU/Linux will encourage you to do just that.

14. THE CHRISTIAN FOSS MOVEMENT

What most church leaders may not know is that there is a growing community of Christians committed to developing, using, and supporting free and open source software. In the community of hundreds of men and women from various countries and denominational affiliations, you will find Information Technology professionals as well as non-technical users. There is a community of Christians ready, willing, and able to welcome and support their fellow believers.

Many of the free and open source software projects for the Church have been around for some time. Thousands of people have been using these programs from their beginnings. Yet, finding these projects has not been easy. Even if you know where to search, and the terms to use, you could overlook some of the projects. That has changed dramatically.

A few of the Christian FOSS community's websites have been mentioned throughout this book. We'll get to know these a little better. We'll also discover a few more sites that have not yet been mentioned. The community has no format structure, and yet there is a collaborative effort among the members of all the websites to accomplish various projects.

We'll examine the philosophical debate as it exists within the Christian Community. It exists in the larger secular community as well. The debate is much the same, regardless of one's faith – or lack thereof. Thus it makes the most sense to view the debate as it applies to Christians. This author's own viewpoint should be quite clear. Enlightening debate is most welcome.

We'll also consider how Christians might come together to help make free and open source software an even better alternative to the standard proprietary fare. While developers are needed in several areas, even non-developers can participate in a big way. If you can write simple instructions, share a program with a friend, or actively help others (after learning a bit yourself), you can contribute to the community.

Christian FOSS Websites

The Freely Project is working to change this. While Freely has a help desk, members of this web forum are organizing at the local level, both for advocacy and for technical support. Members are starting to act as local coordinators to help spread the word to Christians in their own areas. Some are simply working to develop marketing materials. And some are reaching out to local Linux Users Groups to find others willing to help provide technical support locally.

The freely Project offers an Internet Relay Chat (IRC) channel on the well-known Freenode IRC service. IRC is a fun way to chat "live" over the Internet. Users not familiar with IRC will need an IRC client and connect to Freenode. From there it is simply a matter of typicing *#freely* to join the channel. With members spread around the world, users will likely find someone on #freely nearly anytime of the day. The IRC Help Homepage (www.irchelp.org) offers help in getting started with IRC.

Freely members often try out applications that could be useful to ministries and offer evaluations of them in the forums. The Freely Project recently connected with TechMission and will soon distribute their free software CD, based on the GNU CD. Freely has been featured in articles on NewsForge and SearchEnterpriseLinux.com.

Ben Thorp, Freely's webmaster, lives in Scotland and works for IBM. He recognized the need for people to advocate free and open source software in their churches, and setup Freely for the task. When he's not busy managing Freely, he's usually tinkering with various GNU/Linux distributions and applications. He is also moderator of one of the forums at JustLinux.org.

Open Source Ministry is a web forum where technology and ministry meet. Ministry leaders can work with technologists to solve problems. While OS Ministry members tend to be more Windows oriented, the idea of GNU/Linux – and open source software in general – is very much alive. OS Ministry offers news about the Christian FOSS community and about open source software in general, especially as it pertains to the community.

OS Ministry is headed by Bob Brown, a Florida minister. He participates in the Christian Webmasters website and is working to develop the "Holy Scripters" (a play on HotScripts) website for Christian software developers. Bob is instrumental in helping to bring up the news portal for the Christian FOSS community.

The Christian Open Development Network is a site devoted to launching Christian software development projects. Developers can meet and help each other. Users can find projects that may not be listed elsewhere (though most are). CODN is undergoing a transition in the site design. The new design is much more polished and easier to navigate.

The ChristianSource – Free Software and Linux Users Group (CS-FSLUG) is an e-mail list where Christians can discuss technical issues, as well as faith and politics. Because not everyone enjoys the political or theological debates, posters usually preface these with "PD" or "TD" in the subject line of the e-mail. Users can then filter out the non-technical messages if desired. Prayer requests are another feature that makes CS-FSLUG a great list.

CS-FSLUG is moderated by Tim Butler, a Christian businessman who runs the Open For Business website and several others. Tim also offers web hosting to those who ask. A number of the members of CS-FSLUG are regular writers for OFB. Members hail from Israel and Japan, as well as The Netherlands.

Linux 4 Christians (L4C) is another e-mail list that, at one time, had united with CS-FSLUG, and has now become its own list again. It has a different character, and seems to be mostly American in nature, though a few folks of other nationalities are also part of the list. Discussions tend to be less political and somewhat less technical than the CS-FSLUG list.

L4C members have been behind efforts to develop a Christian-oriented GNU/Linux distribution. The man behind the Christian Linux Live CD project recently put the project on the shelf to focus on his family. Apologetix, which appears to be a Morphix-based distribution seems to be progressing slowly. Lyricue's developer created a Morphix CD with the lyrics projection project. L4C is moderated by Linc Fessenden a former pastor in Michigan. Linc is currently the UNIX editor for TechChristian.com, a Christian technical news portal.

A new project, due to launch this Summer (2005), is CrazyChurch.com. It is not so much software as music, lyrics, and other materials produced by a group of five churches in Cincinnati, Austin, Detroit, and just outside of Atlanta. All material will be released gratis and under Creative Commons licenses. This essentially applies the concepts of free software to other creative works. Such an effort is vital to the Christian community, especially in light of efforts to further destroy the balance of freedom that America's copyright laws were designed to maintain.

According to Brian Wells, the Teaching Pastor at Crossroads Community Church, CrazyChurch.com is based on II Corinthians 5:13. The Church discovered Creative Commons through *Wired Magazine* and Steve Wetzel, a long-time member of the FOSS community, who recently stepped up to head the North American operations and world-wide sales for *Free Software Magazine*. Crossroads (www.crossroadscommunity.net) has always made its Sunday service CDs available gratis, and is simply extending this idea to its other materials.

Wells believes that Christians can learn and accomplish much more following the principles of free software, as opposed to commercializing the Gospel and restricting the ability to share information. The authors have the liberty to choose which Creative Commons License they will release their works under. While there have been a number of questions pertaining to rights, Crossroads has been able to point people to the Creative Commons website to answer their concerns.

The various application and OS distribution projects also have communities of their own. Since we have discussed these in Chapter 11, it is not necessary to repeat that information here. You will find their web forums and e-mail lists within their respective web pages.

The Philosophical Dialogue

While Christians have been involved in the free and open source software movement from the onset, and the movement has grown, we need to be aware that not all Christians are motivated by the ideological motives that have inspired Richard Stallman and the Free Software Foundation. Some believers see parallels between free software and spiritual freedom. Others simply like the development model and/or the technical merits of free and open source software.

Our purpose here is primarily to explore the ethical arguments involved in software licenses. The rest of this book has been devoted to the technical and budgetary advantages of using free software. The views expressed here are primarily the author's, and some in the Christian FOSS community dissent. However, the goal of the exploration is to invite the Church to a dialogue about freedom.

Free software does not save, Jesus does. As far as we know, no Christian has adopted or developed a "theology of computing", and the views in the community cannot be called "core beliefs". Nor are Christians confusing technology with theology. The moral arguments for using free software should be understood as the application of God's love where software licenses are concerned.

While Stallman makes a mockery of religion with his "church of EMACS", and has humorously designated himself "Saint I*gnu*cious", Christians might still learn something of value. Stallman expresses at least two concerns that Christians should share. The first is that prohibiting sharing is a greater wrong than sharing illegally. The second concern is with the subjection of users to developers' "rulership".

In examining the first concern, we should note that the opposing viewpoint counters that everyone, including Christians, has the right to charge a fee they deem appropriate, and to restrict others' use of software. It is true that people have a right to charge an appropriate fee for services rendered, for products made, and for software developed. It is also true that a business model that attempts to translate non-physical "material" (software) into physical property is bound to run into significant challenges.

Because the nature of software is so different from physical material, it must be treated differently from a business perspective. In our attempts to fit a round peg (software) into a square hole (physical property), we have now made the act of sharing a criminal act for those who agree to the terms of most proprietary software. Not that sharing is immoral, but we make it so in the terms of a proprietary license.

Consider Jesus' healing of a man and a woman on the Sabbath day (two separate incidents). His acts of mercy stirred a great deal of anger in the Jews of His day – at least among the leadership. He responded by asking whether it was lawful to do good, or to do evil on the Sabbath. From this lesson, we can discern that not all laws (or their interpretation) are moral or good. In turn, a license that criminalizes sharing would seem to violate the Law of Love in a similar manner.

It seems that any business manager worth their salt should be able to find a more appropriate business model to build on. Several companies have made quite a handsome profit selling free software. However, many of them also throw proprietary software into the mix, thus creating potential issues for those who wish to use free software. The GNU GPL and other licenses do allow developers to sell software on a per user basis. However, such licenses potentially also mean that people can share the software they purchase.

Stallman considers the illegal act of sharing to be nevertheless morally proper. This would certainly be no different than Jesus healing on the Sabbath, which was also viewed as illegal. However, an even better idea is for Christians to avoid using software tainted by a license that criminalizes sharing. Likewise, Christian developers would be better off not licensing software under such terms.

One other aspect of this issue is that non-free licenses pit users against each other. Because users cannot share, a world of haves and have-nots continues. Free software levels the playing field while still feeding developers. Thus, in a very real (current) situation, an unemployed sister-in-Christ is being helped using free software. In return, she is offering services to the supporting ministry. She has the ability to continue her employment search, and her children can do their homework. This would be significantly more difficult using non-free software.

The CrazyChurch.com effort is inspired by Lawrence Lessig (lawyer and author of several books on copyright law and freedom) and Creative Commons. They believe in sharing – and allowing others to share. This freedom is fundamental to the growth of the church. The prevailing view is "we have received freely, we should give freely". This attitude stands in stark contrast to the stand that some Christians have taken, along with Hollywood, toward strengthening so-called "copyright protection".

The other concern Stallman had was the user's ability to modify the software they used. The question to ask is whether we have a right to prohibit others from modifying their software. To me, the answer lies in the fact that the person who owns the computer ought also has the right to own and control the software that runs it. After all, without that software, all a person has is a heap of metal and plastic. Since some proprietary software will stop running if not registered, users may find they cannot even boot their systems (Windows XP is only one example).

A person can modify practically any physical tool they purchase. They may need special skills or the money to pay someone else to make the modifications, but they still have the right. Yet, because proprietary software vendors are attempting to control how users use the software on their own computers (round peg in square hole effect), they have decided to withhold the source code that enables such modifications to be made.

Even freeware (proprietary software that can be shared) creates this forced dependence upon the developer, due to the terms of most freeware licenses. Users are free to share, but not to modify the software. Witholding the source code subjects the user to the vendor's control. Whereas copyright doctrine attempts to balance the developers' rights against the social benefit, proprietary licenses force the users to be completely dependent upon the developer. It may be legal in a number of countries to treat people this way, but it is not necessarily right.

A few problems with this kind of control present themselves. For one, this kind of control exhibits little or no respect for the users. When we subject users to developer control we crush creativity and force (or build) dependence. That is never right. While we are all subject to the authority of the government, it's limited control over us does not crush our creativity or build dependence. An excellent program may be undermined by poor business management or other factors. When the vendor goes out of business, no one will be able to continue development.

The free software community is one where people don't run around snooping under the hood of your computer, trying to snoop out the "pirated" software. That's because there is no "need" to "pirate" software in a free software community. After all, the software is free. To be sure, when people discover that someone is using free software in an improper manner, they usually get compliance without the legal wrangling found elsewhere.

In addition to the primary concerns of Stallman, which harmonize with Christian values, many Christians - regardless of their view of the philosophical issues - nonetheless see in free software several parallels to biblical themes. The Freely Project takes its name from the scripture, "Freely you have received, freely give" (Mt. 10:8). Some see free software as a parallel to the free gift of grace, but not on the same level.

There are comparisons of proprietary software to the Old Covenant (restrictive and stuffy), and free software to the New Covenant (liberating and refreshing). Free software may be compared to a technological "promised land". This picture of free software depicts Christians (or people in general) being delivered from the oppressive EULAs and into a land where they can build on what already exists. While their spiritual value is questionable, these comparisons certainly illustrate the nature of the relationship between free software and non-free software.

Some Christians, along with their secular counterparts argue that all software – regardless of the license involved – is neutral. Others counter that any license that prohibits access to the underlying source restricts free access to information, and thus puts the users at a disadvantage. In other words, while proprietary software forces dependence on the developer, free software promotes independence. For this very reason, the Peruvian congressman sought to prohibit the use of proprietary software in government agencies.

Those who argue that licenses are neutral claim that, by ignoring technology on the basis that we disagree with the license terms, we miss out on that technology. On the other hand this argument ignores the harm done by the developers who made the technology proprietary. From a development perspective, the code used must be duplicated cleanly by those who wish to use such technology elsewhere (thus increasing development costs). From a relationship perspective, the user is forced into dependence upon the developer.

Should Christians be more interested in technology than in moral values, as expressed in the terms of a license? All developers have a choice in how they license their software. It seems appropriate, from a biblical perspective, to choose license terms that coincide with biblical principles. Thus, including terms in a software license that prohibit sharing or modifications would be a travesty. Users should likewise be conscientious about using software accompanied by a license that undermines their freedom.

Those Christians who see free software as a moral imperative are not alone. Richard Stallman has communicated with this author (2004) – and with the

World Association for Christian Communication in 2002 – that Christians should be pushing the adoption of free software. The importance of this statement should not be lost on those unfamiliar with a man well-known for his devout atheism. Additionally, many politicians and citizens of numerous countries now seek to implement free software in lieu of proprietary software.

Given that many atheist geeks openly attack Christians in the Internet forums (even just for mentioning the word "church"), Stallman's warm welcome is refreshing. O. Hobart Mowrer once accused the Church of selling her birthright (counseling) for a meal of psychological pottage. Stallman similarly seems to be wondering where the Church is at the precise moment in history that we most risk returning to the Dark Ages. According to Stallman:

"I've always believed that free software is a moral imperative for Christian communicators. Christians, and people of other faiths, cannot morally condone the control of human knowledge or the limiting of development that proprietary software causes." (http://www.wacc.org.uk/wacc/publications/media_actio n/archive/245_jul_2002/stallman_free_software_is_a_mo ral_imperative_for_christians).

Whatever your own views, it is important that the Christian Church wrestle with questions like this. We should all acknowledge that, to some extent, we are still maturing in our understanding of our faith. As long as we can continue to respect each other in the midst of such debates, we will surely be fighting "the good fight". Therefore, let us demonstrate grace and love, even as we strive to answer, as Stallman has sought to do, the question of morality and software licenses.

How Christians Can Improve FOSS

Free and open source software has much to offer. Yet much remains to be done. You and your church can help support FOSS in a number of ways – even if you choose not to migrate. Many Christians only use GNU/Linux or BSD. Many others would like to, but feel stuck with proprietary systems for a variety of reasons. Perhaps, if we examine some of the issues that prevent people from migrating wholesale to a FOSS platform, you will be better able to see how you can help.

One major problem with GNU/Linux is the lack of commercial retailers providing GNU/Linux computers. Wal-Mart now sells computers with Linspire installed. However, most retailers are not providing GNU/Linux as an optional operating system. Many that do offer GNU/Linux as a choice don't make it as obvious as they could. You have to know that they offer a choice, before you know to look.

One salesperson I spoke with at Best Buy kept trying to insist that GNU/Linux is a geek toy. However, if they sold computers with GNU/Linux pre-installed, those computers would have all the advantages of most Windows systems. Most users don't install Windows – it comes pre-installed on the computer they purchase. If a GNU/Linux system were configured similarly, then the Windows computers would lose their advantage.

We mentioned in "The Compatibility Challenge" that one major issue facing GNU/Linux users is hardware support. The reason is that many manufacturers only support Windows or Mac systems. At least part of the reason for their lack of support is due to misunderstandings about legal issues. Another issue seems to be the perceived lack of GNU/Linux users. This is a major reason why many GNU/Linux users continue to dual-boot.

None of the proprietary church management software developers have any plans to develop open source versions of their software, or even proprietary versions that run on open source operating systems. This issue affects churches that have invested hundreds or thousands of dollars into proprietary database solutions. Migrating from these solutions can be costly. Developers that choose to support free and open source software platforms open doors for themselves.

Christians can work together to address these issues. Well-organized e-mail campaigns would be very useful. When you visit your favorite retailer, let them know you want more options, as far as operating systems are concerned. Let them know that you deserve a choice, and that they should be willing to inform you of alternatives to their current offerings. Encourage them to inform you about GNU/Linux.

One area that deserves special attention is that of Bible translations that cannot currently be used with free and open source Bible study applications. For instance, the New International Version module is locked, as the developers do not have permission to make it available to the community. The New American

Standard Bible will soon be available for a small fee, thanks to the efforts of the CrossWire Bible Society.

These translations are available to other, freeware applications for a small fee, and thus should also be made available to the free and open source software community in the same manner. English translations are not the only ones subject to such challenges. A number of modern Bible translations and scholarly texts are locked, due to a lack of permission from the copyright holders. These folks should be encouraged to make such materials available, even if for a fee.

Even if you or your ministry choose not to use free and open source software, you could certainly encourage manufacturers, retailers and copyright holders to open their doors to the Christian FOSS community. A concern for fairness and customer service should prevail. No one is asking the vendors to "give away" anything, but simply to make their products, software, and services available to those who use a different platform.

Users can learn about a good e-mail campaign from the FreeBSD folks, who orchestrated a successful campaign to obtain permission to distribute proprietary hardware drivers with FreeBSD. All that is needed are a few Christians willing to produce a good e-mail template and help recruit people to send out the e-mail. Please note that the Sword Project used to ask for help with e-mailing Bible publishers. In some cases, this may be unproductive, and they have ceased this campaign.

Another way Christians can help improve free and open source software is by participating in the application development projects. Even if you are not a programmer, developers need feedback from users to help them improve their software. Applications that are not specific to Christians need similar involvement from users. If you are able to write, produce some step-by-step instructions for projects that have little documentation available.

I hope you have enjoyed your introduction to the Christian FOSS community. Feel free to visit and participate – in any way you can – with your brothers and sisters in Christ. I hope, too, that you will join in the dialogue – and seek to engage others – regarding the moral issues involving software licenses. And finally, regardless of what you think of what I have said here, I do hope you will help to improve the free and open source software community – both for Christians and for the larger secular community.

15. THE GUIDE TO GNU/LINUX DISTRIBUTIONS

Software frequently consists of a number of different files that are packed into a single compressed file, and then *distributed* across the Internet, or by CD and other media. Thus, the term *distribution* could refer to a single program or an entire operating system, together with its included programs. Thus GNU/Linux can be distributed by any number of people, including you.

Which distribution you choose depends on your situation. One of the advantages of GNU/Linux is that you do have a choice. If one distribution doesn't suit your needs, another very likely will. Some organizations distribute GNU/Linux commercially, while others distribute it as a non-profit enterprise. Both have advantages and disadvantages that churches will want to consider as they explore the idea of migrating to this extremely flexible operating system.

One of the major differences between distributions is their approach to package management. Software is usually "packaged" for installation on the computer, and distributions have a few different ways to handle that. Red Hat developed the "Red Hat Package Manager", or RPM. Debian's "apt" is extremely popular. In fact, there is now a utility called "Apt for RPM" that users of RPM-based distributions are deploying. Most distributions are said to be "RPM-based" or "Debian-based".

Most distributions offer CD images over the Internet. Those with broadband Internet connections can download the software and burn the "ISO" image to CD. Once on CD, you just reboot your computer to install GNU/Linux, or run the live distribution right off the CD. You can also pass these out to others. Exploring the various BSD distributions is an exercise left to the reader. Web links are included in the Resources section of this book.

Note: Many of the distributions listed here include non-free software in their selection of packages. The Free Software Foundation rejects the use of non-free software. Thus they only recommend Ututo-e and Dynebolic, which only contain free software. So far,

Debian

Debian is a non-profit distribution. It is perhaps best known for being a real challenge to install, but extremely easy to maintain. Debian also has a reputation as the most stable distribution available. Debian has three branches – unstable, testing, and stable. You can use whichever branch you want, but no packages enter the stable branch until all known security and stability issues have been resolved. Several companies and non-profit groups have developed customized (usually much easier to use) distributions based on Debian. Debian does make non-free software available.

Fedora Core

Fedora Core is Red Hat's "community edition", and is actually the future Red Hat Linux (their corporate enterprise offering). Red Hat is probably the most widely used in the American corporate scene. Because of this, many GNU/Linux users already have skills with Fedora Core. There may even be some Red Hat Certified Engineers in your local area. The Red Hat certification is highly respected and sought after. Red Hat developed the Red Hat Package Management (RPM) in use by a number of GNU/Linux distributions, and focuses on the GNOME desktop environment. I've received confusing information on the inclusion of non-free software in Fedora Core.

Mandrake

Mandriva Linux is the result of the recent merger between Mandrake (France) and Connectiva (Brazil), and is also pretty popular in the the United States. Mandriva, like Red Hat, is an RPM-based distribution, albeit with a focus on the KDE desktop. Mandriva offers a variety of solutions for a wide range of users, and especially aims for the "Linux newbie" market – folks who are unfamiliar with GNU/Linux.

SUSE

SUSE was a German company until Novell purchased them. Novell offers SUSE Linux to both the enterprise market and the SOHO market. SUSE Linux Professional is the SOHO edition, and is inexpensive enough for most home users. Novell has recently released the Novell Linux Desktop, a new corporate workstation distribution. SUSE is another very popular distribution that is respected for its security and its support for a wide range of hardware. SUSE includes Main Actor and other non-free software in its "boxed" editions.

Slackware

Slackware is considered to be the "first" GNU/Linux distribution. It is, perhaps, the only one managed by a single individual. Slackware tends to attract the more experienced users, though they manage to entice some of the newbies as well. Slackware has a long and noble history, and should serve most churches well.

Xandros Desktop

The folks behind Xandros used to be the developers behind the now defunct Corel Linux. They took Debian GNU/Linux, customized it heavily to look a lot like Windows, and have put a tremendous amount of effort into getting it to work pretty much like a Windows system. Because it is Debian underneath, it offers most of the advantages of that system, albeit, minus some of the issues that could trouble some new users. Xandros uses non-free software to enhance its distribution.

Linspire

Linspire used to be known as Lindows, and is very much like Xandros. Linspire, however, is aimed more at the home user market, and offers a high level of compatibility with Windows multi-media formats. Linspire offers a wide range of commercial options, and makes a great choice for home and SOHO users. Linspire is sold pre-installed on computers through Wal-Mart's website. Linspire includes non-free software (StarOffice, etc.) as part of its offering.

Knoppix

Knoppix is a live CD distribution based on Debian. The idea is that it runs from the CD, thus making it easy for users to get a feel for GNU/Linux without installing it to their hard drive. Users who like it can then install it. Some Windows administrators keep a copy around to help them rescue their Windows systems. Readers will want to determine whether Knoppix includes non-free software. It probably includes it or makes it available.

Morphix

Morphix is based on Knoppix, but allows users to customize the distribution to suit their needs. For instance, users can choose between GNOME, KDE, and Xfce-oriented CD images. Users can customize the apps they use, which makes it perfect for setting up a demonstration CD, featuring a particular application set. Morphix can be installed as well.

Mepis

Mepis is a Debian-based distribution operating out of West Virginia, and is perhaps best known for its hardware support and ease of use. It is a commercial distribution, but users can still download the base ISO images for free. In reality, the fee for Mepis is very reasonable. Because it is Debian-based, Mepis likely makes non-free software available.

Ubuntu

Ubuntu is based on Morphix, and is meant to be very easy to install. One can install Ubuntu on a relatively slow 450 MHz computer in just one hour. It will attempt to connect to the Internet and update itself. Quite a few people run Ubuntu on laptops, as it is so easy and offers most of the basic software they use. By default, this distribution will overwrite your hard drive during installation, which is a bit unusual. Just be careful to manually partition your hard drive if you want to leave Windows on your system. Ubuntu does make non-free software available via its repository, but does not support it. It is up to users to ensure compliance with non-free licenses.

Gentoo

Gentoo, named for the breed of penguins, is a very different GNU/Linux system. Gentoo is designed to provide users with a system optimized for their specific hardware. It is notoriously slow to install, but once complete, offers unbridled speed and excellent stability. Gentoo uses a tool called *Portage*, which both maintains and builds software packages for your PC.

Apologetix

Apologetix is another Morphix derivative, albeit headed up by a Christian from Mississippi. This distribution is in development, and will likely include many of the tools churches would use most.

Ichthux

Ichthux is a recent project, formed by the several developers, each attempting a decent distribution on their own. So far, this appears to be an effort to develop a custom Debian Distribution. This approach means that developers can bring the project up to speed in a short time, while simultaneously providing users with the widest range of software and solid support.

http://ichthiux.free.fr/wikini/wakka.php?wiki=Main

Jesux

You may run into references to Jesux. This was revealed to be a hoax a fairly long time ago, but some people still don't know that. Essentially, it's made out to be a fundamentalist Christian distribution. The link below will take the curious to the site (still up, as of the time of this publication).

http://www.geocities.com/ResearchTriangle/Node/4081/

RESOURCES

Although there are numerous resources, I have here included the most pertinent and useful to the uninitiated. I have also refrained from listing books geared toward specific distributions. Most of the web sites below sites offer links to other useful and more specific sites. I have also included a listing of the most recently available prices of the operating systems and applications discussed in this book.

Taran Rampersad has done an excellent job of discussing the differences between Microsoft Office and OpenOffice.org. Rampersad's article article was published at NewsForge (www.newsforge.com/software/04/03/27/0134204.shtml), and responds to a marketing document that apparently used to exist on the Microsoft web site. He points out the differences in system requirements, functionality, and interoperability.

Books

IDG Books Worldwide, Sybex, Wrox Press, and Osbourne McGraw Hill publish excellent books, in my experience. I understand O'Reilly is a solid publisher as well, although I have not actually read any of their books.

Installing and Administering Linux
Author(s): Linda McKinnon   Publisher: John Wiley & Sons

Installing and Administering Linux
Author(s): Linda McKinnon   Publisher: John Wiley & Sons

Linux : The Complete Reference (Complete Reference)
Author(s): Richard Petersen   Publisher: Osborne McGraw-Hill

Linux Administration: A Beginner's Guide
Author(s): Steve Shah   Publisher: McGraw-Hill Professional Publishing

Linux in the Workplace
Author(s): Publishers of Linux Journal   Publisher: No Starch Press

Professional Linux Deployment
Author(s): Michael Boerner   Publisher: Wrox Press Inc

StarOffice™ for Linux® Bible
Author(s): Jacek Artymiak   Publisher: IDG Books Worldwide

Taming OpenOffice.org Writer 1.1
Author(s): Jean Hollis Weber   Publisher: Weberwoman's Wrevenge

OOo Switch: 501 Things You wanted to know about switching to OpenOffice.org from Microsoft Office.
Author(s): Tamar E. Granor   Publisher: Hentzenwerke Publishing

Magazines & Internet Media

Free Software Magazine
www.freesoftwaremagazine.com
Audience: General
Publisher: Tony Mobily
Format: Print/Web
Cover Price: $4.95/month

Sys Admin
Audience: System Administrators
Publisher: Miller Freeman
Format: Print/Web
Cover Price: $39/Year

Linux Journal
www.linuxjournal.com
Audience: General
Publisher: Specialized Systems Consultants
Format: Print/Web
Cover Price: $22/Year

Linux Magazine
www.linux-mag.com
Audience: General
Publisher: Linux Magazine
Format: Print
Cover Price: $34.95/Year

Tux Magazine
www.tuxmagazine.com
Audience: Newbies
Format: Web based
Cover Price: no charge

SearchEnterpriseLinux.com
Audience: Technical Managers
Publisher: TechTarget
Format: Web-based

Linux Gazette
Audience: General
Publisher: Specialized Systems Consultants
Format: Downloadable tar gzip file
Cover Price: Free Monthly e-zine.

Web Sites

General Information

The Free Software Foundation	www.fsf.org
Open Source Initiative	www.opensource.org
The Free Standards Group	www.freestandards.org
Creative Commons	www.creativecommons.org
Filesystem Hierarchy Standard	www.pathname.com/fhs/
Linux On-Line	www.linux.org
Linux Central	www.linuxcentral.com
Linux International	www.li.org
Linux Hardware.Net	www.linuxhardware.net
Linux Hardware.Org	www.linuxhardware.org
Linux HCL	www.tldp.org/HOWTO/Hardware-HOWTO/

Help Sites

The Linux Documentation Project	www.tldp.org
HowTo Forge	www.howtoforge.com
Just Linux	www.justlinux.org
Linux Questions	www.linuxquestions.org
OpenOffice.org Help	documentation.OpenOffice.org

Security Sites

Linux Security   www.linuxsecurity.com

Privoxy   www.privoxy.org

DansGuardian   www.dansguardian.org

Distribution Websites

DistroWatch   www.distrowatch.com

Linux ISO   www.linuxiso.org

Novell, SUSE Linux
www.novell.com

Red Hat   www.redhat.com

Fedora Core (by Red hat)   www.fedoracore.org

Mandriva (formerly Mandrake/Connectiva)   www.mandriva.com

Debian   www.debian.org

Xandros   www.xandros.com

Linspire   www.linspire.com

Slackware   www.slackware.org

Gentoo   www.gentoo.org

Morphix   www.morphix.org

Ubuntu   www.ubuntu.org

Mepis   www.mepis.com

FreeBSD   www.freebsd.org

OpenBSD   www.openbsd.org

NetBSD   www.netbsd.org

Applications

Appgen's (My Books)	www.appgen.com
Code Weavers	www.codeweavers.com
Scribus	www.scribus.net
Info Central	www.infocentral.org
Church Info	www.churchinfo.org
CHADDB	chaddb.sourceforge.net
Lyricue	www.adebenham.com/lyricue
OpenLP	www.openlp.org
OpenSong	www.opensong.org
CrossWire/Sword Project	www.crosswire.org

Prices

Prices used in this document are based on website pricing info as of 18 April 2005, and therefore may be outdated by the time you read this. (Author's note: prices do not appear to have changed significantly over the last year.)

Microsoft Windows 2003 Server (Small Business) = $620

(Standard) = $999

http://www.compusa.com/products/products.asp?N=0&Ntt=windows%20server&Ntk=All&Nty=1&D=windows%20server

Microsoft Windows XP Professional (Upgrade) = $170 (Full) = $300

http://www.officemax.com/max/solutions/product/prodBlock.j
sp?BV_UseBVCookie=yes&expansionOID=-
536884233&prodBlockOID=536950572

Microsoft Office Standard (Upgrade) = $239 (Full) = $399

http://www.officemax.com/max/solutions/search/search.jsp?B
V_UseBVCookie=yes&searchType=product&searchString=Micro
soft+Office&searchBtn.x=23&searchBtn.y=10

Capterra – Church Management Software List

http://www.capterra.com/church-management-software

Powerchurch = $395 w/90 Days support (usually costs $595)

www.powerchurch.com

Church Pro = $200-$500, depending on church needs

www.churchpro.com

Roll Call = $59-$1695, depending on # of records

http://www.bythebook.com/order1.html

Church Windows = $475 for 100 families

http://www.churchwindows.com/

Servant Keeper = $250 for small churches – over $1000

Logos Management = $500-$5000

http://www.logoslbe.com/main.cfm?id=100

Faithful Steward = $199

http://www.church-software.com/fs/index.htm

Red Hat Linux Workstation = $179   Enterprise Server = $349

http://www.redhat.com/software/rhel/purchase/index.html

Fedora Core (by Red Hat) = Gratis

http://fedora.redhat.com/

Mandriva Linux (Advanced) = $85
http://store.mandriva.com/index.php?currency=USD&osCsid=7
787e6fcb3f0c7dcd96333d7458e3c19

SUSE Linux Professional 9.3 = $100 (Full) $60 (Upgrade/Student)

http://www.suse.com/us/private/products/suse_linux/i386/pri
ces.html

Xandros Desktop Business Edition = $129   (5-Pack) = $495

http://www.xandros.com/products/shopping.html

GLOSSARY

Client-Server – A technology in which one computer or program provides services to other computers (workstations) or programs (clients).

Database – program that stores data, allowing users to add, edit, and retrieve that data.

Desktop – A graphical shell. The starting point from which users launch applications. GNU/Linux makes use of "virtual" desktops to allow users to better organize their tasks.

GNU (GNU's Not UNIX) – a recursive acronym that plays on the proprietary nature of most UNIX systems. It is a set of tools that, with the Linux kernel, comprise a complete, free operating system.

Kernel – The operating system's kernel provides the interface between the application software and the computer's hardware.

JDBC (Java DataBase Connector) – allows people using Java technology to connect to databases.

Newbie – A novice user, especially those new to the GNU/Linux community. Several GNU/Linux distributions attempt to make it easy for newbies to learn about GNU/Linux systems.

ODBC (Open Database Connector) – allows people using ODBC-capable applications to connect to standard SQL databases.

OASIS (Organization for the Advancement of Structured Information Standards) – is a non-profit, international consortium that creates interoperable industry specifications based on public standards such as XML and SGML.

OSIS (Open Scripture Information Standard) – is an XML schema for marking up scripture and related text, part of an "open scripture" initiative composed of translators, publishers, scholars, software manufacturers, and technical experts who are coordinated by the Bible Technologies Group.

Protocol – A set of rules for communicating across a network. Just as humans use different protocols for business and church, computers require different protocols for accomplishing different tasks. For instance, the HyperText Transfer Protocol (HTTP) is used for displaying documents marked up with HTML. On the other hand, files are most commonly transferred using the File Transfer Protocol (FTP).

PNG (Portable Network Graphics) – An open graphics format designed to replace the proprietary GIF format.

Shell (see "User Interface")

SQL (Structured Query Language) – The standard relational database technology in use today. Microsoft SQL Server, Oracle, Informix, MySQL, and PostGreSQL are the most common databases in use. MySQL and PostGreSQL are the two most popular open source databases.

User Interface (command-line and graphical) – Also called a "shell". The point of a user's interaction with a computer. From the Command-Line interface (CLI), a user is prompted to type commands. In a graphical user interface (GUI) users click on icons to execute commands.

THE GNU GENERAL PUBLIC LICENSE (GPL)

Version 2, June 1991

Copyright (C) 1989, 1991 Free Software Foundation, Inc. 59 Temple Place, Suite 330, Boston, MA 02111-1307 USA

Everyone is permitted to copy and distribute verbatim copies of this license document, but changing it is not allowed.

Preamble

The licenses for most software are designed to take away your freedom to share and change it. By contrast, the GNU General Public License is intended to guarantee your freedom to share and change free software--to make sure the software is free for all its users. This General Public License applies to most of the Free Software Foundation's software and to any other program whose authors commit to using it. (Some other Free Software Foundation software is covered by the GNU Library General Public License instead.) You can apply it to your programs, too.

When we speak of free software, we are referring to freedom, not price. Our General Public Licenses are designed to make sure that you have the freedom to distribute copies of free software (and charge for this service if you wish), that you receive source code or can get it if you want it, that you can change the software or use pieces of it in new free programs; and that you know you can do these things.

To protect your rights, we need to make restrictions that forbid anyone to deny you these rights or to ask you to surrender the rights. These restrictions translate to certain responsibilities for you if you distribute copies of the software, or if you modify it.

For example, if you distribute copies of such a program, whether gratis or for a fee, you must give the recipients all the rights that you have. You must make sure that they, too, receive or can get the source code. And you must show them these terms so they know their rights.

We protect your rights with two steps: (1) copyright the software, and (2) offer you this license which gives you legal permission to copy, distribute and/or modify the software.

Also, for each author's protection and ours, we want to make certain that everyone understands that there is no warranty for this free software. If the software is modified by someone else and passed on, we want its recipients to know that what they have is not the original, so that any problems introduced by others will not reflect on the original authors' reputations.

Finally, any free program is threatened constantly by software patents. We wish to avoid the danger that redistributors of a free program will individually obtain patent licenses, in effect making the program proprietary. To prevent this, we' have made it clear that any patent must be licensed for everyone's free use or not licensed at all.

The precise terms and conditions for copying, distribution and modification follow.

TERMS AND CONDITIONS FOR COPYING, DISTRIBUTION AND MODIFICATION

0. This License applies to any program or other work which contains a notice placed by the copyright holder saying it may be distributed under the terms of this General Public License. The "Program", below,

refers to any such program or work, and a "work based on the Program" means either the Program or any derivative work under copyright law: that is to say, a work containing the Program or a portion of it, either verbatim or with modifications and/or translated into another language. (Hereinafter, translation is included without limitation in the term "modification".) Each licensee is addressed as "you".

Activities other than copying, distribution and modification are not covered by this License; they are outside its scope. The act of running the Program is not restricted, and the output from the Program is covered only if its contents constitute a work based on the Program (independent of having been made by running the Program). Whether that is true depends on what the Program does.

1. You may copy and distribute verbatim copies of the Program's source code as you receive it, in any medium, provided that you conspicuously and appropriately publish on each copy an appropriate copyright notice and disclaimer of warranty; keep intact all the notices that refer to this License and to the absence of any warranty; and give any other recipients of the Program a copy of this License along with the Program.

You may charge a fee for the physical act of transferring a copy, and you may at your option offer warranty protection in exchange for a fee.

2. You may modify your copy or copies of the Program or any portion of it, thus forming a work based on the Program, and copy and distribute such modifications or work under the terms of Section 1 above, provided that you also meet all of these conditions:

a) You must cause the modified files to carry prominent notices stating that you changed the files and the date of any change.

b) You must cause any work that you distribute or publish, that in whole or in part contains or is derived from the Program or any part thereof, to be licensed as a whole at no charge to all third parties under the terms of this License.

c) If the modified program normally reads commands interactively when run, you must cause it, when started running for such interactive use in the most ordinary way, to print or display an announcement including an appropriate copyright notice and a notice that there is no warranty (or else, saying that you provide a warranty) and that users may redistribute the program under these conditions, and telling the user how to view a copy of this License. (Exception: if the Program itself is interactive but does not normally print such an announcement, your work based on the Program is not required to print an announcement.)

These requirements apply to the modified work as a whole. If identifiable sections of that work are not derived from the Program, and can be reasonably considered independent and separate works in themselves, then this License, and its terms, do not apply to those sections when you distribute them as separate works. But when you distribute the same sections as part of a whole which is a work based on the Program, the distribution of the whole must be on the terms of this License, whose permissions for other licensees extend to the entire whole, and thus to each and every part regardless of who wrote it.

Thus, it is not the intent of this section to claim rights or contest your rights to work written entirely by you; rather, the intent is to exercise the right to control the distribution of derivative or collective works based on the Program.

In addition, mere aggregation of another work not based on the Program with the Program (or with a work based on the Program) on a volume of a storage or distribution medium does not bring the other work under the scope of this License.

3. You may copy and distribute the Program (or a work based on it, under Section 2) in object code or executable form under the terms of Sections 1 and 2 above provided that you also do one of the following:

a) Accompany it with the complete corresponding machine-readable source code, which must be distributed under the terms of Sections 1 and 2 above on a medium customarily used for software interchange; or,

b) Accompany it with a written offer, valid for at least three years, to give any third party, for a charge no more than your cost of physically performing source distribution, a complete machine-readable copy of the corresponding source code, to be distributed under the terms of Sections 1 and 2 above on a medium customarily used for software interchange; or,

c) Accompany it with the information you received as to the offer to distribute corresponding source code. (This alternative is allowed only for noncommercial distribution and only if you received the program in object code or executable form with such an offer, in accord with Subsection b above.)

The source code for a work means the preferred form of the work for making modifications to it. For an executable work, complete source code means all the source code for all modules it contains, plus any associated interface definition files, plus the scripts used to control compilation and installation of the executable. However, as a special exception, the source code distributed need not include anything that is normally distributed (in either source or binary form) with the major components (compiler, kernel, and so on) of the operating system on which the executable runs, unless that component itself accompanies the executable.

If distribution of executable or object code is made by offering access to copy from a designated place, then offering equivalent access to copy the source code from the same place counts as distribution of the source code, even though third parties are not compelled to copy the source along with the object code.

4. You may not copy, modify, sublicense, or distribute the Program except as expressly provided under this License. Any attempt otherwise to copy, modify, sublicense or distribute the Program is void, and will automatically terminate your rights under this License. However, parties who have received copies, or rights, from you under this License will not have their licenses terminated so long as such parties remain in full compliance.

5. You are not required to accept this License, since you have not signed it. However, nothing else grants you permission to modify or distribute the Program or its derivative works. These actions are prohibited by law if you do not accept this License. Therefore, by modifying or distributing the Program (or any work based on the Program), you indicate your acceptance of this License to do so, and all its terms and conditions for copying, distributing or modifying the Program or works based on it.

6. Each time you redistribute the Program (or any work based on the Program), the recipient automatically receives a license from the original licensor to copy, distribute or modify the Program subject to these terms and conditions. You may not impose any further restrictions on the recipients' exercise of the rights granted herein. You are not responsible for enforcing compliance by third parties to this License.

7. If, as a consequence of a court judgment or allegation of patent infringement or for any other reason (not limited to patent issues), conditions are imposed on you (whether by court order, agreement or

otherwise) that contradict the conditions of this
License, they do not excuse you from the conditions
of this License. If you cannot distribute so as to
satisfy simultaneously your obligations under this
License and any other pertinent obligations, then as
a consequence you may not distribute the Program at
all. For example, if a patent license would not
permit royalty-free redistribution of the Program by
all those who receive copies directly or indirectly
through you, then the only way you could satisfy both
it and this License would be to refrain entirely from
distribution of the Program.

If any portion of this section is held invalid or
unenforceable under any particular circumstance, the
balance of the section is intended to apply and the
section as a whole is intended to apply in other
circumstances.

It is not the purpose of this section to induce you
to infringe any patents or other property right
claims or to contest validity of any such claims;
this section has the sole purpose of protecting the
integrity of the free software distribution system,
which is implemented by public license practices.
Many people have made generous contributions to the
wide range of software distributed through that
system in reliance on consistent application of that
system; it is up to the author/donor to decide if he
or she is willing to distribute software through any
other system and a licensee cannot impose that choice.

This section is intended to make thoroughly clear
what is believed to be a consequence of the rest of
this License.

8. If the distribution and/or use of the Program is
restricted in certain countries either by patents or
by copyrighted interfaces, the original copyright
holder who places the Program under this License may
add an explicit geographical distribution limitation
excluding those countries, so that distribution is
permitted only in or among countries not thus

excluded. In such case, this License incorporates the limitation as if written in the body of this License.

9. The Free Software Foundation may publish revised and/or new versions of the General Public License from time to time. Such new versions will be similar in spirit to the present version, but may differ in detail to address new problems or concerns.

Each version is given a distinguishing version number. If the Program specifies a version number of this License which applies to it and "any later version", you have the option of following the terms and conditions either of that version or of any later version published by the Free Software Foundation. If the Program does not specify a version number of this License, you may choose any version ever published by the Free Software Foundation.

10. If you wish to incorporate parts of the Program into other free programs whose distribution conditions are different, write to the author to ask for permission. For software which is copyrighted by the Free Software Foundation, write to the Free Software Foundation; we sometimes make exceptions for this. Our decision will be guided by the two goals of preserving the free status of all derivatives of our free software and of promoting the sharing and reuse of software generally.

NO WARRANTY

11. BECAUSE THE PROGRAM IS LICENSED FREE OF CHARGE, THERE IS NO WARRANTY FOR THE PROGRAM, TO THE EXTENT PERMITTED BY APPLICABLE LAW. EXCEPT WHEN OTHERWISE STATED IN WRITING THE COPYRIGHT HOLDERS AND/OR OTHER PARTIES PROVIDE THE PROGRAM "AS IS" WITHOUT WARRANTY OF ANY KIND, EITHER EXPRESSED OR IMPLIED, INCLUDING, BUT NOT LIMITED TO, THE IMPLIED WARRANTIES OF MERCHANTABILITY AND FITNESS FOR A PARTICULAR PURPOSE. THE ENTIRE RISK AS TO THE QUALITY AND PERFORMANCE OF THE PROGRAM IS WITH YOU. SHOULD THE PROGRAM PROVE DEFECTIVE, YOU ASSUME THE COST OF ALL NECESSARY

SERVICING, REPAIR OR CORRECTION.

12. IN NO EVENT UNLESS REQUIRED BY APPLICABLE LAW OR AGREED TO IN WRITING WILL ANY COPYRIGHT HOLDER, OR ANY OTHER PARTY WHO MAY MODIFY AND/OR REDISTRIBUTE THE PROGRAM AS PERMITTED ABOVE, BE LIABLE TO YOU FOR DAMAGES, INCLUDING ANY GENERAL, SPECIAL, INCIDENTAL OR CONSEQUENTIAL DAMAGES ARISING OUT OF THE USE OR INABILITY TO USE THE PROGRAM (INCLUDING BUT NOT LIMITED TO LOSS OF DATA OR DATA BEING RENDERED INACCURATE OR LOSSES SUSTAINED BY YOU OR THIRD PARTIES OR A FAILURE OF THE PROGRAM TO OPERATE WITH ANY OTHER PROGRAMS), EVEN IF SUCH HOLDER OR OTHER PARTY HAS BEEN ADVISED OF THE POSSIBILITY OF SUCH DAMAGES.

END OF TERMS AND CONDITIONS

How to Apply These Terms to Your New Programs

If you develop a new program, and you want it to be of the greatest possible use to the public, the best way to achieve this is to make it free software which everyone can redistribute and change under these terms.

To do so, attach the following notices to the program. It is safest to attach them to the start of each source file to most effectively convey the exclusion of warranty; and each file should have at least the "copyright" line and a pointer to where the full notice is found.

One line to give the program's name and a brief idea of what it does. Copyright (C) <year> <name of author>

This program is free software; you can redistribute it and/or modify it under the terms of the GNU General Public License as published by the Free Software Foundation; either version 2 of the License, or (at your option) any later version.

This program is distributed in the hope that it will
be useful, but WITHOUT ANY WARRANTY; without even the
implied warranty of MERCHANTABILITY or FITNESS FOR A
PARTICULAR PURPOSE. See the GNU General Public
License for more details.

You should have received a copy of the GNU General
Public License along with this program; if not, write
to the Free Software Foundation, Inc., 59 Temple
Place, Suite 330, Boston, MA 02111-1307 USA

Also add information on how to contact you by
electronic and paper mail.

If the program is interactive, make it output a short
notice like this when it starts in an interactive
mode:

Gnomovision version 69, Copyright (C) year name of
author Gnomovision comes with ABSOLUTELY NO WARRANTY;
for details type `show w'. This is free software, and
you are welcome to redistribute it under certain
conditions; type `show c' for details.

The hypothetical commands `show w' and `show c'
should show the appropriate parts of the General
Public License. Of course, the commands you use may
be called something other than `show w' and `show c';
they could even be mouse-clicks or menu items--
whatever suits your program.

You should also get your employer (if you work as a
programmer) or your school, if any, to sign a
"copyright disclaimer" for the program, if necessary.
Here is a sample; alter the names:

Yoyodyne, Inc., hereby disclaims all copyright
interest in the program `Gnomovision' (which makes
passes at compilers) written by James Hacker.

signature of Ty Coon, 1 April 1989 Ty Coon, President
of Vice

This General Public License does not permit

incorporating your program into proprietary
programs. If your program is a subroutine
library, you may consider it more useful to
permit linking proprietary applications with the
library. If this is what you want to do, use the
GNU Library General Public License instead of
this License.

THE OPEN SOURCE

DEFINITION

Version 1.9

*The indented, italicized sections below appear as annotations to the Open Source Definition (OSD) and are **not** a part of the OSD.*

Introduction

Open source doesn't just mean access to the source code. The distribution terms of open-source software must comply with the following criteria:

1. Free Redistribution

The license shall not restrict any party from selling or giving away the software as a component of an aggregate software distribution containing programs from several different sources. The license shall not require a royalty or other fee for such sale.

Rationale: *By constraining the license to require free redistribution, we eliminate the temptation to throw away many long-term gains in order to make a few short-term sales dollars. If we didn't do this, there would be lots of pressure for cooperators to defect.*

2. Source Code

The program must include source code, and must allow distribution in source code as well as compiled form. Where some form of a product is not distributed with source code, there must be a well-publicized means of obtaining the source code for no more than a reasonable reproduction cost–preferably, downloading via the Internet without charge. The source code must be the preferred form in which a programmer would modify the program. Deliberately obfuscated source code is not allowed. Intermediate forms such as the output of a preprocessor or translator are not allowed.

Rationale: We require access to un-obfuscated source code because you can't evolve programs without modifying them. Since our purpose is to make evolution easy, we require that modification be made easy.

3. Derived Works

The license must allow modifications and derived works, and must allow them to be distributed under the same terms as the license of the original software.

Rationale: The mere ability to read source isn't enough to support independent peer review and rapid evolutionary selection. For rapid evolution to happen, people need to be able to experiment with and redistribute modifications.

4. Integrity of The Author's Source Code

The license may restrict source-code from being distributed in modified form only if the license allows the distribution of "patch files" with the source code for the purpose of modifying the program at build time. The license must explicitly permit distribution of software built from modified source code. The license may require derived works to carry a different name or version number from the original software.

Rationale: Encouraging lots of improvement is a good thing, but users have a right to know who is responsible for the software they are using. Authors and maintainers have reciprocal right to know what they're being asked to support and protect their reputations.

*Accordingly, an open-source license **must** guarantee that source be readily available, but **may** require that it be distributed as pristine base sources plus patches. In this way, "unofficial" changes can be made available but readily distinguished from the base source.*

5. No Discrimination Against Persons or Groups

The license must not discriminate against any person or group of persons.

Rationale: In order to get the maximum benefit from the process, the maximum diversity of persons and groups should be equally eligible to contribute to open sources. Therefore we forbid any open-source license from locking anybody out of the process.

Some countries, including the United States, have export restrictions for certain types of software. An OSD-conformant license may warn licensees of applicable restrictions and remind them that they are obliged to obey the law; however, it may not incorporate such restrictions itself.

6. No Discrimination Against Fields of Endeavor

The license must not restrict anyone from making use of the program in a specific field of endeavor. For example, it may not restrict the program from being used in a business, or from being used for genetic research.

Rationale: The major intention of this clause is to prohibit license traps that prevent open source from being used commercially. We want commercial users to join our community, not feel excluded from it.

7. Distribution of License

The rights attached to the program must apply to all to whom the program is redistributed without the need for execution of an additional license by those parties.

Rationale: This clause is intended to forbid closing up software by indirect means such as requiring a non-disclosure agreement.

8. License Must Not Be Specific to a Product

The rights attached to the program must not depend on the program's being part of a particular software distribution. If the program is extracted from that distribution and used or distributed within the terms of the program's license, all parties to whom the program is redistributed should have the same rights as those that are granted in conjunction with the original software distribution.

Rationale: This clause forecloses yet another class of license traps.

9. License Must Not Restrict Other Software

The license must not place restrictions on other software that is distributed along with the licensed software. For example, the license must not insist that all other programs distributed on the same medium must be open-source software.

Rationale: *Distributors of open-source software have the right to make their own choices about their own software.*

Yes, the GPL is conformant with this requirement. Software linked with GPLed libraries only inherits the GPL if it forms a single work, not any software with which they are merely distributed.

10. License Must Be Technology-Neutral

No provision of the license may be predicated on any individual technology or style of interface.

Rationale: *This provision is aimed specifically aimed at licenses which require an explicit gesture of assent in order to establish a contract between licensor and licensee. Provisions mandating so-called "click-wrap" may conflict with important methods of software distribution such as FTP download, CD-ROM anthologies, and web mirroring; such provisions may also hinder code re-use. Conformant licenses must allow for the possibility that (a) redistribution of the software will take place over non-Web channels that do not support click-wrapping of the download, and that (b) the covered code (or re-used portions of covered code) may run in a non-GUI environment that cannot support popup dialogues.*

OPEN SOFTWARE LICENSE

V. 2.1

This Open Software License (the "License") applies to any original work of authorship (the "Original Work") whose owner (the "Licensor") has placed the following notice immediately following the copyright notice for the Original Work:

Licensed under the Open Software License version 2.1

1) **Grant of Copyright License.** Licensor hereby grants You a world-wide, royalty-free, non-exclusive, perpetual, sublicenseable license to do the following:

- to reproduce the Original Work in copies;

- to prepare derivative works ("Derivative Works") based upon the Original Work;

- to distribute copies of the Original Work and Derivative Works to the public, with the proviso that copies of Original Work or Derivative Works that You distribute shall be licensed under the Open Software License;

- to perform the Original Work publicly; and

- to display the Original Work publicly.

2) **Grant of Patent License.** Licensor hereby grants You a world-wide, royalty-free, non-exclusive, perpetual, sublicenseable license, under patent claims owned or controlled by the Licensor that are embodied in the Original Work as furnished by the Licensor, to make, use, sell and offer for sale the Original Work and Derivative Works.

3) **Grant of Source Code License.** The term "Source Code" means the preferred form of the Original Work for making modifications to it and all available documentation describing how to modify the

Original Work. Licensor hereby agrees to provide a machine-readable copy of the Source Code of the Original Work along with each copy of the Original Work that Licensor distributes. Licensor reserves the right to satisfy this obligation by placing a machine-readable copy of the Source Code in an information repository reasonably calculated to permit inexpensive and convenient access by You for as long as Licensor continues to distribute the Original Work, and by publishing the address of that information repository in a notice immediately following the copyright notice that applies to the Original Work.

4) **Exclusions From License Grant.** Neither the names of Licensor, nor the names of any contributors to the Original Work, nor any of their trademarks or service marks, may be used to endorse or promote products derived from this Original Work without express prior written permission of the Licensor. Nothing in this License shall be deemed to grant any rights to trademarks, copyrights, patents, trade secrets or any other intellectual property of Licensor except as expressly stated herein. No patent license is granted to make, use, sell or offer to sell embodiments of any patent claims other than the licensed claims defined in Section 2. No right is granted to the trademarks of Licensor even if such marks are included in the Original Work. Nothing in this License shall be interpreted to prohibit Licensor from licensing under different terms from this License any Original Work that Licensor otherwise would have a right to license.

5) **External Deployment.** The term "External Deployment" means the use or distribution of the Original Work or Derivative Works in any way such that the Original Work or Derivative Works may be used by anyone other than You, whether the Original Work or Derivative Works are distributed to those persons or made available as an application intended for use over a computer network. As an express condition for the grants of license hereunder, You agree that any External Deployment by You of a Derivative Work shall be deemed a distribution and shall be licensed to all under the terms of this License, as prescribed in section 1(c) herein.

6) **Attribution Rights.** You must retain, in the Source Code of any Derivative Works that You create, all copyright, patent or trademark

notices from the Source Code of the Original Work, as well as any notices of licensing and any descriptive text identified therein as an "Attribution Notice." You must cause the Source Code for any Derivative Works that You create to carry a prominent Attribution Notice reasonably calculated to inform recipients that You have modified the Original Work.

7) **Warranty of Provenance and Disclaimer of Warranty.** Licensor warrants that the copyright in and to the Original Work and the patent rights granted herein by Licensor are owned by the Licensor or are sublicensed to You under the terms of this License with the permission of the contributor(s) of those copyrights and patent rights. Except as expressly stated in the immediately proceeding sentence, the Original Work is provided under this License on an "AS IS" BASIS and WITHOUT WARRANTY, either express or implied, including, without limitation, the warranties of NON-INFRINGEMENT, MERCHANTABILITY or FITNESS FOR A PARTICULAR PURPOSE. THE ENTIRE RISK AS TO THE QUALITY OF THE ORIGINAL WORK IS WITH YOU. This DISCLAIMER OF WARRANTY constitutes an essential part of this License. No license to Original Work is granted hereunder except under this disclaimer.

8) **Limitation of Liability.** Under no circumstances and under no legal theory, whether in tort (including negligence), contract, or otherwise, shall the Licensor be liable to any person for any direct, indirect, special, incidental, or consequential damages of any character arising as a result of this License or the use of the Original Work including, without limitation, damages for loss of goodwill, work stoppage, computer failure or malfunction, or any and all other commercial damages or losses. This limitation of liability shall not apply to liability for death or personal injury resulting from Licensor's negligence to the extent applicable law prohibits such limitation. Some jurisdictions do not allow the exclusion or limitation of incidental or consequential damages, so this exclusion and limitation may not apply to You.

9) **Acceptance and Termination.** If You distribute copies of the Original Work or a Derivative Work, You must make a reasonable effort under the circumstances to obtain the express assent of recipients to the terms of this License. Nothing else but this License

(or another written agreement between Licensor and You) grants You permission to create Derivative Works based upon the Original Work or to exercise any of the rights granted in Section 1 herein, and any attempt to do so except under the terms of this License (or another written agreement between Licensor and You) is expressly prohibited by U.S. copyright law, the equivalent laws of other countries, and by international treaty. Therefore, by exercising any of the rights granted to You in Section 1 herein, You indicate Your acceptance of this License and all of its terms and conditions. This License shall terminate immediately and you may no longer exercise any of the rights granted to You by this License upon Your failure to honor the proviso in Section 1(c) herein.

10) **Termination for Patent Action.** This License shall terminate automatically and You may no longer exercise any of the rights granted to You by this License as of the date You commence an action, including a cross-claim or counterclaim, against Licensor or any licensee alleging that the Original Work infringes a patent. This termination provision shall not apply for an action alleging patent infringement by combinations of the Original Work with other software or hardware.

11) **Jurisdiction, Venue and Governing Law.** Any action or suit relating to this License may be brought only in the courts of a jurisdiction wherein the Licensor resides or in which Licensor conducts its primary business, and under the laws of that jurisdiction excluding its conflict-of-law provisions. The application of the United Nations Convention on Contracts for the International Sale of Goods is expressly excluded. Any use of the Original Work outside the scope of this License or after its termination shall be subject to the requirements and penalties of the U.S. Copyright Act, 17 U.S.C. Â§ 101 et seq., the equivalent laws of other countries, and international treaty. This section shall survive the termination of this License.

12) **Attorneys Fees.** In any action to enforce the terms of this License or seeking damages relating thereto, the prevailing party shall be entitled to recover its costs and expenses, including, without limitation, reasonable attorneys' fees and costs incurred in connection with such action, including any appeal of such action. This section shall survive the termination of this License.

13) **Miscellaneous.** This License represents the complete agreement concerning the subject matter hereof. If any provision of this License is held to be unenforceable, such provision shall be reformed only to the extent necessary to make it enforceable.

14) **Definition of "You" in This License.** "You" throughout this License, whether in upper or lower case, means an individual or a legal entity exercising rights under, and complying with all of the terms of, this License. For legal entities, "You" includes any entity that controls, is controlled by, or is under common control with you. For purposes of this definition, "control" means (i) the power, direct or indirect, to cause the direction or management of such entity, whether by contract or otherwise, or (ii) ownership of fifty percent (50%) or more of the outstanding shares, or (iii) beneficial ownership of such entity.

15) **Right to Use.** You may use the Original Work in all ways not otherwise restricted or conditioned by this License or by law, and Licensor promises not to interfere with or be responsible for such uses by You.

This license is Copyright (C) 2003-2004 Lawrence E. Rosen. All rights reserved. Permission is hereby granted to copy and distribute this license without modification. This license may not be modified without the express written permission of its copyright owner.

INDEX

214

V

Virus   **20, 51, 76, 79, 82, 91, 94p., 129**

W

Webmin   **63**

Win4Lin   **48**

Windows   **1pp., 5pp.,** 9, **18p., 21, 43, 45pp., 52, 54pp., 58, 60pp., 68,** 70, **72pp.,** 75, **76p., 83, 85pp.,** 91p., **96, 103,** 105, **112, 114, 120, 122,** 125p., **130, 133pp., 137, 139pp., 151,** 157, 162, **163, 170pp., 180p.**

Windows 2000   **6, 76**

Windows 3.11 **60**

Windows 95   **5p.**

Windows 98   21, 48

Windows Compatibility Software   **31, 35p., 48**

Windows XP   21

WINE **48**

Women   **109, 149**

Word   **17, 47, 49, 65, 87**

WorkPlace   **48**

Workstation   **2, 4p., 46, 51, 80, 135p., 141, 170, 182**

Workstations   **5, 137, 183**

World Association for Christian Communication   161

Writer   **17, 49, 52, 65, 107**

X

Xandros   **48,** 71, **76, 78,** 135, **170,** 179, **182**

XFce   **56pp., 130, 136**

Ximian   **46**

XMMS   **61, 66**

Y

Yast   **43, 62pp., 70, 81**

Yellow Dog   **93**

YOU   **63, 194p., 205**

Z

Zaurus **19**

Zip   **44**

About Don Parris

Don is a bi-vocational minister and former business owner. He holds a Master of Theology degree from Lighthouse Christian College, and leads Oakdale (formerly known as Matheteuo) Christian Fellowship, a house church in Charlotte, North Carolina. He has served as Minister of Christian Education and as Director of Ministries for two churches in the Charlotte area.

Don previously operated The Parris Group, a computer services firm. He is an advanced, mostly self-taught user of Windows and GNU/Linux. He has been using GNU/Linux since Red Hat Linux 5.2. In addition to his experience as a Bible Study teacher, Don has taught a number of basic computer courses, mostly to low-income students.

Don has been busy advocating the use of free and open source software in Christian ministries. He works closely with The Freely Project and Open Source Ministry on advocacy issues. He has contributed a small amount of documentation to the JSword project, and designed CHADDB, the **Ch**urch **Ad**ministration **D**atabase. He is available as a speaker for ministries and other organizations interested in using free and open source software.

Oakdale Christian Fellowship has a number of computers, which run various flavors of GNU/Linux. Aside from SUSE, Oakdale has deployed Ubuntu, Mepis, and is currently testing Ututo-e. These computers serve as a lab when not in classroom use. Oakdale is currently sponsoring a family in their transition to GNU/Linux from the Windows platform.

www.ingramcontent.com/pod-product-compliance
Lightning Source LLC
Chambersburg PA
CBHW051232050326
40689CB00007B/886